ANTHEM PUBLISHING

Hebrews:
The Epistle of the Diathéké:

Geerhardus Vos

ANTHEM PUBLISHING
A Division of re:SOURCE DIGITAL PUBLISHING
Formatted and Printed in the United States of America
Digital edition also available.
ISBN: 9798693952942

Preface

The great legacy of the Princeton theologians is one of the great gifts that the modern church has received. Though their approach to scholarship and the words they chose are less familiar to us, a study based on close reading of their work yields limitless fruit—especially in an era so prone to theological wandering.

The work of these theologians constantly calls us back to the Bible and to examine the text faithfully, in detail, and with a heart devoted to God's revelation in Jesus Christ communicated to us through the Bible.

Hebrews: The Epistle of the διαθήκη is pristine example of this emphasis. Vos pinpoints this word because it plays a key role in Hebrews and yet is relatively absent elsewhere in the New Testament. By examining its various occurrences and the concepts similar to it throughout Scripture, Vos illuminates its role in the salvation-historical (heilgeschicte) process and to provide lucid biblical analysis for any student of the Bible. We hope you enjoy this study and hope you will explore the other titles available from Geerhardus Vos, especially our <u>Vos collection</u> featuring his most important contributions.

—Anthem

Contents

ANTHEM PUBLISHING

Hebrews:
The Epistle of the διαθήκη:
A Two Part Thematic Examination

Geerhardus Vos

Part I

Originally published in *The Princeton Theological Review*, 1915.

In the following article an attempt is made to trace the part which the Greek διαθήκη plays in the teaching of the Epistle to the Hebrews.

We leave the Greek word untranslated, because it is in part with the problem of its proper translation that we are concerned and it appears best not to prejudice the question. We notice first of all that Hebrews is the only New Testament document in which the concept and the term *diatheke* appear with any degree of prominence. In the teaching of our Lord we meet with the idea only once, in the institution of the Supper. More frequently it occurs with Paul, in Romans (9:4; 11:27), 2 Corinthians (3:6, 14), Galatians (3:15, 17; 4:24), Ephesians (2:12), altogether nine times in six contexts. In Luke's writings we find it, apart from the institution of the Supper, once in the Gospel (1:72), and twice in the Acts (3:25; 7:8). Once also it is met with in the Revelation of St. John (11:19). This makes sixteen instances of its occurrence outside of Hebrews. Over against this stand seventeen occurrences in Hebrews alone. In other words in this single Epistle the conception is more frequent than in all the rest of the New Testament writings put together.

Both these facts require an explanation—the relative quiescence of the idea in the New Testament as a whole, no less than its sudden activity in Hebrews. It seems strange at first that a conception which plays so dominant a rôle in the

Old Testament and so strongly colors the representation of religion there should have found so little employment in the later stage of revelation. The cause is usually sought in this, that other ideas like the Kingdom of God and the Church have forced it into the background and taken its place. But this is rather a fuller statement of the problem, and only in so far of help towards the solution, than the solution itself. For the question persists: Why did other ideas, and precisely these ideas, become so dominant as to relegate the *diatheke*-idea to semi-oblivion? To this question the answer can only be found in the momentous change to which in the development of redemption and revelation the general character of religion became subject. Through the coming of the Messiah and the accomplishment of His work the people of God received a Messianic organization; their whole constitution and manner of life became determined by their relation to the Christ. Now the Old Testament idea of the *berith*, had in the long course of its history, scarcely come as yet into fructifying contact with the Messianic hope of Israel. Therefore at the dawn of the new dispensation it was not prepared to take the lead in the great rearrangement of doctrinal values characteristic of this epoch. While inherently not incapable of entering upon an organic union with the Messianic point of view, yet on the surface it did not suggest or invite such an interrelation. It will be remembered that the great prophecy of Jeremiah concerning the new *berith* which Jehovah will make with Israel in the future is not Messianically oriented. A definite, specific

3

historical situation was required to draw this ancient idea into the service of the new Messianic outlook created by the appearance of Jesus and the accomplishment of His work.

In general we may say that such a situation was bound to arise as soon as the consciousness of the original and unique blessings conferred by Christianity led to a comparison between the present stage of redemptive attainment and the past. It is the retrospective, comparative mode of thinking applied from the exalted standpoint of Christian privilege and seeking to reach an adequate apprehension of the rich content of the latter by placing it over against the lower pre-Christian stage of redemption and revelation that has in most cases resurrected the *diatheke*-idea and brought it into new significance. This is entirely in accord with the first use made by Jeremiah of the idea in connection with the future. The future order of things appears to the prophet as a *berith* because he pointedly compares it with and exalts it above the past and present order of things. Partly in dependence on this prophetic passage, but also with a broad historical comparison between the era introduced by the sacrifice at Sinai in the time of Moses and the era introduced by His own sacrifice, our Lord speaks of the latter in the institution of the Supper as a new *diatheke*. Again it is under the influence of the same comparative train of thought when Paul in 2 Corinthians 3 represents his apostolic ministry as a service connected with a *diatheke*, the new *diatheke*, not of the letter but of the Spirit, over against which he places the ministry of Moses as subservient to another *diatheke*, embodied in the Old Testament Scriptures. It may be observed in passing that the Apostle here by way of metonymy applies the term *diatheke* to the Scriptures themselves, since he alternates the phrase "the reading of Moses" with the other phrase "the reading of the old *diatheke*" (verses 14 and 15). This is the first instance of the literary usage of the term so familiar to us in the names Old Testament and New Testament as designations of the two canons of Scripture. The fact should not be overlooked, however, that even this literary usage has its roots in the Hebrew Scripture since *berith* there appears as a synomym of *thora*, law, and consequently like the latter comes to designate the written code as a rule of faith and practice. On the other hand there is no proof that the literary turn given by Paul to the phrase "old *diatheke*" had anything to do with the apocalyptic custom of representing the alleged oracular utterances of ancient Scriptural personages as their "testament" *e.g.* "The Testaments of the Twelve Patriarchs." The other source is plainly indicated because Paul in the same sense speaks of the reading of Moses and the reading of the old *diatheke*.

With equal clearness the comparative view-point as inducing the emergence of the conception can be observed in Galatians 4. Here Paul speaks of two contrasting διαθῆκαι, *i.e.* two great religious systems operating by diverse methods and with opposite results, the one a Hagar-

diatheke, geographically associated with Mount Sinai, the other a Sarah-*diatheke* having its local center in the heavenly Jerusalem. There is a difference between this and 2 Corinthians 3 insofar as there the old and the new were contrasted in their original God-willed and God-given character, whilst here in Galatians the Sinaitic-Hagar-*diatheke* is the old system as perverted by Judaism. But the comparative manner of handling the idea is the same in both passages and in both cases is alike responsible for its introduction.

These are the only instances in the New Testament, apart from Hebrews, where the term is applied to the Christian dispensation. In all other cases its use is purely retrospective, the reference being to the ancient theocratic order of affairs. Coming with the result obtained to Hebrews, it is not difficult to see that here likewise the motive of comparison between the old and the new religious systems very largely underlies the prominent use made of the *diatheke*-idea. In view of the specific purpose which the writer pursues it was inevitable that this idea should spring into prominence. We need not at this point discuss the problem why the author of Hebrews institutes such a careful and elaborate comparison between the old theocratic and the new fabric of religion. The old view, still widely taken of the matter, is that the readers of the Epistle, by reason of their Jewish descent and Old Testament associations, perhaps also their proximity to the still existing temple-service, were personally and practically interested in the comparative merits of the two systems contrasted and in need of fresh assurance in regard to the superiority of the Christian religion to that of Judaism. In recent times this older view has been steadily losing ground and it has been widely assumed that the interest of both author and readers in the Old Testament mode of religion was produced by theoretical rather than by practical considerations, the Mosaic institutions being used merely as a foil to set off the excellence of Christianity as the supreme and final religion. As observed, it is immaterial for our present purpose to take sides in this debate for on either view of the question the comparative structure of the Epistle's argument stands out in bold relief. For whatever purpose he did it, the writer plainly wanted to contrast the old dispensation with the new. For doing this he needed a common denominator, and since the old order was to all intents a *berith*, a διαθήκη, the new order had, in order to be commensurable with the other, to be likewise represented under the same aspect. The only other form of which the writer might have availed himself to carry through the comparison was that of law and legal organization. The Epistle actually in a few passages approaches this point of view (7:12 "the priesthood being changed, there is made of necessity a change also of law"; 8:6 Christ is "Mediator of a better covenant which has been legally enacted upon better promises"). But it is easy to see that, however admirably this might suit the Mosaic order of things, the Christian order could not be adequately described as a new law, since in its fundamental aspects it transcends the category of law and since precisely in this supra-legal character consists a large part of that superiority of the Christian state which the author is intent upon bringing out. The exigency, therefore, of the comparative view-point, here no less than in the case of our Lord and of Paul, brought the *diatheke*-idea to the front and incorporated it in the new Christian thought-system.

While this explanation of the prominence of the idea in Hebrews is undoubtedly correct so far as it goes, it does not quite satisfy. One cannot help feeling that after all the writer's attitude of mind towards the conception is a somewhat different one from that of Jesus and Paul. With Jesus and Paul the term is taken up for the momentary purpose of comparison and, having served its purpose, allowed to drop out of sight. It exerts no further influence upon the structure of thought. Even what it expresses might have been expressed in other terms without essentially altering the content of truth. It is not so in Hebrews. Here the *diatheke*-idea shapes and colours the doctrinal outlook to a considerable degree and in important respects. Though the writer may at first have called it into requisition for formal purposes merely, yet we can clearly perceive how in his hands it outgrows this subsidiary function and leaps to the rank of a valuable concept doctrinally suggestive and stimulating to the author's own mind, fruitful and pregnant with new potentialities of thought. Therefore to take this idea out of Hebrews would have quite different results than would follow its elimination from the teaching of our Lord and Paul. Through its removal the inner organism of the Epistle's teaching would be injured and significant lines and shades of its doctrinal complexion obliterated from our view. Its revelation-value would suffer a real impairment.

In order to show that this is so it will be necessary to face a problem which up to this point we have purposely refrained from injecting into the discussion. The problem concerns the meaning of the word *diatheke* in its religious usage. The two renderings "covenant" and "testament" have long contended for the supremacy. Of the thirty-three times in which the word occurs in the New Testament the Authorized Version renders it twenty-one times by "covenant" and twelve times by "testament." This already marks a considerable preponderance of "covenant" over "testament". In the Revised Version this preponderance becomes far greater, for here of the twelve instances of "testament" only two remain, so that the proportion according to the Revisers stands thirty-one to two. When the Revised Version was made, therefore, *i.e.* more than three decades ago, the meaning "covenant" seemed in a fair way of dislodging the other rendering from the English Bible. This preference for "covenant" was undoubtedly due in large measure to the presumption in its favor created by the Old Testament. In the Hebrew Scriptures the meaning "testament" has no standing at all. Proceeding on the legitimate principle that in a matter of this kind harmony and continuity may be assumed to exist between the two canons of Scripture, the translators naturally felt bound to retain "covenant" so long as the import and context of a passage did not absolutely exclude it. At the same time there seems to have persisted in the mind of the Revisers a feeling that their verdict in favor of "covenant" was not absolutely final. They appear not to have been enough convinced to rule the rendering "testament" entirely out of court. In each of the cases where they substitute "covenant" for the "testament" of the Authorized Version they give in the margin "testament" as a possible alternative. And not only this, they offer of their own accord the same marginal alternative in nine additional cases, where the Authorized Version had already "covenant". That is to say, even where the Authorized Version and the Revised Version agreed in favoring "covenant", the Revisers deem it necessary to warn the reader that the possibility of the word meaning "testament" must be reckoned with. As a matter of fact, then, the Revision, so far from decisively settling the question, has by accentuating in so many instances the double possibility of rendering, placed the old problem more than ever in evidence.

That this was a wise suspension of judgment seems to be borne out by the recent course of investigation. If at the time of the Revision "covenant" was gaining on "testament," the roles have now been reversed. The opinion of writers who of late years have occupied themselves with the subject has been steadily moving away from the rendering "covenant" to the other translation. Even where a stop is made at the half-way station of "disposition", "arrangement" and the specialized meaning of "testament" not insisted upon, the idea of "covenant" is none the less deliberately rejected as inapplicable. In this point Riggenbach and Deissmann and Behm and Lohmeyer all agree. This remarkable veering around of opinion is the result of a new method of approach to the problem. The linguistic method of settling such a question is at present in the ascendant. The interest of scholars is no longer directed towards giving *diatheke* a meaning which shall keep it in touch or harmony with Old Testament precedent but exclusively towards explaining it from the common, secular Hellenistic *usus loquendi* at the time when the Septuagint and the New Testament were produced. The discovery and utilisation for New Testament science of the papyri and ostraka has made it possible to turn "the light from the Orient," as upon so many other things, also upon the *diatheke*-idea. The Septuagint has been studied with the distinct thought in mind that it should not be read in dependence upon the Hebrew original but treated as a linguistically self-explanatory document. Even the classical meaning of the word, in distinction from the later Hellenistic usage, has been exhaustively traced through its several stages and thus a complete history of the development of διαθήκη in the Greek language from its earliest emergence down to the eve of the New Testament period and to a much later point, has been laid before us.

As a result of all this investigation and discussion it is now claimed by prominent scholars that *diatheke* in Hellenistic Greek bore and could bear no other meaning than that of "testament" and consequently must have been meant in the same sense by the Septuagint translators and the New Testament writers, at least if we assume that these desired to be understood by their readers. Now, since nothing is more certain than that such a conception of *berith* as a "testament" is utterly foreign to the intent of the Hebrew Scriptures, the position taken implies that the Seventy by translating as they did committed a stupendous blunder, and that in two directions; first by importing a false idea into the Old Testament, secondly by failing to reproduce the correct idea there found. So far as the Septuagint is concerned, this might not seem in itself such a very serious matter. We do not ascribe to the Greek Old Testament infallibility; its text is not to us a canonical text. None the less the matter is of considerable importance. The seriousness arises from the connection between the Septuagint and the New Testament. For the New Testament writers inherited this blunder from the Seventy. They also took *diatheke* as "testament" and labored under the same delusion that the *berith* of the Hebrew Scriptures was to be so understood. In other words

there is involved in the case a huge misunderstanding of the
Old Testament on the part of the writers of the New.

The advocates of the new view, however, are not much
troubled by this. They care as little for the inspiration and
infallibility of the New Testament, as we would be apt to
care for the inerrancy of the Septuagint. But not only are
they not seriously disturbed by the matter, they are
enthusiastically elated over it. To their mind it is a most
extraordinary case of religious good coming out of linguistic
evil. To the cause of religion the Greek translators rendered
by their mistake a signal service. The Old Testament idea of
the *berith*, that is of the "covenant", was an idea of very
inferior worth and questionable associations, belonging to a
low plane of religious development. It is at bottom
unworthy of the relation between God and man, ideally
considered, to think of the two as contractually united. And,
on the other hand, the idea of God issuing a testament, that
is making sovereign disposal in matters of religion is an
inherently noble conception. Although, therefore, the
procedure of the Septuagint cannot be justified
philologically, we are invited to hail its result as a great
religious gain. Deissmann speaks about it in the following
words: "The Bible which conceives of the relation between
God and man as a divine 'testament' moves, with Paul and
Augustine, on a higher plane than the Bible (*i.e.* the Hebrew
Scriptures) which represents God as making contracts."[1]

---

[1] Die Hellenisierung des Semitischen Monotheismus, p. 175, quoted by Lohmeyer, p. 96.

And Behm delivers himself to the same effect: "The act of
making a contract with its synergism gives way" (through the
rendering of the Septuagint) "to the monergism of the
sovereign pronouncement by which God prescribes His will
to man, either commanding or promising gifts, by way of
law or of grace."[2]

What shall we say to these things? In our humble opinion
the conclusion which these scholars arrive at is a mixture of
error and truth, both as regards its linguistic side and as
regards the comparative estimate they put upon the religious
value of the two ideas of "covenant" and "testament" as
exponential of the spirit of the older and later Scriptures
respectively. To begin with the linguistic aspect of the
question, the whole antithesis between *berith* as meaning
"covenant" and *diatheke* as meaning "testament" is, in the
absoluteness with which it is here advocated, untenable and
in the highest degree misleading. To charge the Old
Testament, on account of its *berith*-conception, with the
doctrine that God synergistically enters into contracts with
man is a gross injustice. The fact is that, preoccupied with
their own specialty of Hellenistic Greek, the scholars who
make this charge have failed to keep up with the progress of
Old Testament science. Even if *diatheke* meant "testament"
pure and simple in Hellenistic Greek, even then a downright
conflict of the Hebrew Bible with this could only be made

____

[2] Der Begriff Διαθήκη im Neuen Testament, p. 31.

out by giving *berith* the unqualified modern sense of "covenant" *i.e.* of "contract", "agreement". But the adequacy of such a rendering will no longer be upheld by any reputable Old Testament scholar. The sense of "contract", "agreement" does not belong to the essence of the *berith*-conception at all. This does not mean that sometimes in the

Old Testament the *berith* does not appear in the form of an "agreement" between parties and that this may not be an important feature theologically considered. It only means that even in such cases what constitutes the agreement a *berith* is not the two-sidedness but something else which equally well can appear where there is no compact at all. This essential element is the absolute confirmation of the arrangement by means of a religious sanction or ceremony; in other words it is the introduction of the divine factor securing stability that gives to the *berith* its specific character. This is so in the secular *berith* between man and man; but it is from the nature of the case more emphatically so when God is one of the parties entering into an arrangement with man. The circumstance that in virtue of its *berith*-character the arrangements must derive its security not from man but from God has for its necessary result that God where He Himself enters as a party acquires in the transaction a monergistic preponderance which from the outset excludes any idea that He parleyed and contractually negotiated with man in a manner derogatory to His divine position. It thus appears that even where there is a reciprocal relationship the *berith*-aspect of it is the very aspect that keeps it within the bounds of religious dignity and decorum. However bilateral the arrangement may be in its outcome, to God alone belongs the prerogative of initiating it and with Him alone lies the right of determining its content. God never deliberates or bargains with man as to the terms of the *berith* He condescends to enter into. Man may accept voluntarily but can in no wise modify what the sovereign divine will arranges for him. Thus even in the case of an avowed bilateral *berith* there already is seen to exist a balance of monergism on the divine side sufficiently strong to exclude every thought of a contractual procedure unworthy of God. But the *berith* by no means involves such a two-sided arrangement everywhere in the Old Testament. There are numerous instances where the *berith* is wholly one-sided in its import, where man assumes no obligations but is purely receptive in regard to it, in other words, where it amounts to a solemnly sanctioned promise or disposition on the part of God. Such are the *berith* made with Noah and that made with Abraham. Further the frequent equivalence of *berith* and "law" can only be explained on this same principle. The conclusion of the matter, therefore, is that the element of two-sidedness plays a very subordinate role in the Old Testament usage of the term *berith*, and where it does enter, it is very much restricted in scope. The characterization of the Old Testament God as a God making contracts quoted above from Deissmann derives its main support from the rendering "covenant", which, as we have seen, is a very inadequate rendering. If regard is had not to the modern associations of the word "covenant" but to the actual nature of the Biblical *berith* as ascertained by induction, no ground for criticism on that score exists.

But, although the charge of religious inferiority can not justly be brought against the Old Testament *berith*-conception, it may still be asked, whether the charge of linguistic conflict between it and the Greek *diatheke*-idea does not remain? The *diatheke* may not be something higher or more God-worthy than the *berith*, but is it not something specifically different, so that after all the Greek Bible places the idea in a false light and deflects it in a wrong direction? For the answer to this question all depends on what the Greek *diatheke* did actually mean or can have meant to those who equated it to *berith*. If it could mean and did mean nothing else but "a last will," then the conflict with the sense of *berith* lies on the surface and there is no use in trying to argue it away. Nor will it do to say that revelation in its progressive development has the right to modify a conception or even to empty it of its old and fill it with a totally new content. For the later Scriptures in this case are not conscious of such a modification or refilling of the form; on the contrary they profess to employ *diatheke* in such a way as to make it retain its full identity with *berith*. If the identity does not exist, then it is a case of self-delusion such as can hardly be reconciled with the dignity of revelation. The only recourse, therefore, lies in maintaining that the understanding of *diatheke* in Hellenistic Greek was not so absolutely tied down to the sense of "testament" as we are asked to believe. This, we believe, can be maintained, without any stretch of the linguistic conscience. The facts appear to be as follows. Διαθήκη is a derivative of the verb διατίθεσθαι (in the middle voice). The verb means "to order for one's self", "to dispose for one's self". To this general meaning of the verb, the noun must at one time have corresponded in the sense of "arrangement for one's self", "disposition for one's self". But, as is frequently the case with general terms, the noun acquired in course of time a specialized, technical meaning which became so prevalent as to force the original unspecialized signification into the background and practically put it out of use. *Diatheke* became a term of jurisprudence. In this capacity it had two meanings, the one very common, the other, it seems, more rarely employed. The common meaning was that of "testament", "last will", the rarer one that of "treaty", or "mutually obligating law". This specializing development had already run its course before the close of the classical era, so that in Hellenistic Greek *diatheke* had become monopolized by jurisprudence as a technical term. Now the question in hand reduces itself to this, whether in the face of a fixed specialized usage the Septuagint, and in its wake the New Testament writers, could attribute to *diatheke* any other meaning than that of "testament" and still have reasonable ground to believe that in doing this they would be understood by their readers. This question may confidently be answered in the affirmative. It is true that, so far as our knowledge goes, "testament" was the sense commonly connected with the word. But, as already stated, it was not absolutely the only sense; side by side with it, there existed the sense of "treaty" or "mutually obligating law". Even strict adherence to actual usage, therefore, did not compel the translators or the readers to identify a *diatheke* in every case with a "last will". But, what is of more importance, it should further be remembered that the technical meaning acquired by a word may or may not kill the potentialities inherent in the word for reasserting its old use or making new growth in some other direction. A term can become so technical as to lose all adaptability for wider and freer usage. The Latin words "*testamentum*" and "*sacramentum*", and the corresponding English words "testament", "sacrament" are examples of this. In their case the memory of the native sense, which in virtue of their etymology they possessed, has been lost beyond all possibility of resurrection; if any new development occurs it will have to take its point of departure in the technical usage. But it is not necessarily so in every case. A word can become technical and yet a more or less clear consciousness of its original, plastic force and etymological sense may survive enabling the latter to spring into living use whenever the emergencies of expression require it. Now the word *diatheke*, it seems to me, belongs distinctly to this second class. While it had come to mean almost exclusively "testament", the older meaning of

"disposition for one's self" "arrangement for one's self",
which was the parent of the technical use, had only become
momentarily non-active, but could by no means be counted
dead and buried. The stock remained alive and capable of
sending forth a fresh shoot. We must not overlook the
important fact, that, while the noun διαθήκη became
specialized, the corresponding verb διατίθεσθαι did not
share to the same extent in this specializing development. Of
course, it had to follow the noun into the field of
jurisprudence; when διαθήκη meant "testament",
διατίθεσθαι could not help acquiring the sense of "to
make a testament". But there was this difference, that the
noun practically dropped its other meanings whereas the
verb had only gained a new technical adaptation without
detriment to its other usage which remained precisely what
it was before. To the Greek mind διατίθεσθαι did not
necessarily call up the idea of a testamentary transaction; it
could express a disposition or arrangement for one's self in
any other sphere uncolored by the associations of the law-
court or the last will. This, however, could not be without
retroactive influence upon the destinies of the noun. The
etymology of the noun διαθήκη is so perspicuous that it
could never be entirely detached from its parent-stock still
living with unimpaired vigor in the verb. A διαθήκη is so
clearly the result of διατίθεσθαι that whatever the latter
signified, the former also must have remained capable of
signifying anew when occasion sailed for it. If then the

Septuagint translators for good reason thought it desirable to detach the term *diatheke* from the restricted contempory meaning and revert to its original freer force, the technical usage can have presented no insurmountable obstacle.

The next question is, whether the Septuagint, self-interpreted, suggests anywhere that it wants *diatheke* to be understood as "testament." It is *à priori* extremely improbable that this should be the case. A "testament" always carries the implication of the prospective death of the person who makes it. How could such a thought have been applied to God who is throughout the maker of the religious *diatheke?* In the New Testament the *diatheke* as a "last will" is once brought into connection with the sacrifice of Christ, once with the promise of God to Abraham. The former case cannot be put on a line with what the translators of the Septuagint are charged with having perpetrated, because Christ, unlike God, is in His human nature subject to death and can appear in the rôle of testator. The other instance (that in Gal. 3), which actually makes God the testator of the inheritance bequeathed to Abraham, is occasioned by Paul's desire to emphasize the subsequent unchangeableness of the promise. That Paul in an exceptional case and for a concrete reason gives this specific turn to the idea and discounts the element of a contemplated death cannot, of course, give plausibility to the assumption that the Septuagint associated God with the idea of a "last will" on the broadest scale. It ought also to be noticed how in both these New Testament instances the writers do not content themselves with implying the testamental character of the *diatheke*, but take particular pains to call our attention to it so that the import of the word in the context cannot possibly be misunderstood. By accentuating this and using the technical terms of jurisprudence the writers reveal that they are conscious of using the religious *diatheke* in a meaning not normally associated with it. In the Greek Old Testament it is totally different. The translators here give no indication anywhere by their manner of rendering of their desire to have *diatheke* understood as "testament". It may be said that as translators they were precluded from doing this by their dependence on the original from which every allusion to a "last will" in connection with *berith* was absent. Still in other cases the translators of the Septuagint have not been restrained by strict adherence to the Hebrew text from injecting or suggesting their own theological ideas and it is certainly strange that in the numerous cases of their employment of *diatheke* they should have entirely failed to do so. All the more is this to be wondered at, since a direct temptation to underscore the meaning "testament" offered itself in the fact that the Hebrew Scriptures had already associated the two ideas of *berith* and inheritance. Jehovah in virtue of the *berith* gives the inheritance of Canaan to Israel. Of course in the original this combination has nothing whatever to do with the idea of the *berith* as a "last will". But it offered a splendid opportunity for a translator who understood *diatheke* as "testament" to make his understanding of the matter unmistakable. When nowhere a hint to this effect is given, we may safely conclude that the Septuagint had no special proclivity towards identifying the religious *diatheke* with a testament.

If not specifically "testament" what then did the *diatheke* of the Greek translators mean? Would we come nearer to their intent by saying they meant it in the sense of "covenant"? In our opinion an affirmative answer may be given to this in so far as that which we understand by a "covenant" must have entered in a number of cases as a constituent element into their conception of the *berith* and of the *diatheke*, while it is entirely incapable of proof that the idea of a technical testament associated itself for them with these words. They speak sometimes of the *diatheke* in the same way that the Hebrew Bible speaks of the *berith*, as a διαθήκη *with* and *between* persons, and this certainly suggests that it appeared to them as a mutual agreement. There is reason therefore to believe that their idea of the *diatheke* was sufficiently wide and elastic to include the covenantal element. And yet the simple equation of *diatheke* and "covenant" might easily become misleading. The two above-named constructions are not the favorite constructions of the Septuagint. They prefer to speak of a *diatheke* which God makes *towards* men, and this already suggests that the covenantal idea, while not excluded, is in their mind subordinated to and delimited by another idea. This other idea is that of the sovereign prerogative of God to regulate without human interference the redemptive relation that shall exist between Himself and His people, even though this relation may in the outcome partake of the nature of a mutual fellowship and agreement. That the preference given to *diatheke* as a rendering for *berith* actually arises out of consideration for God as the principal factor in the transaction appears from the following: where the *berith* is made between man and man and consists in a mutual agreement, the translators do not employ διαθήκη but συνθήκη, a word exactly corresponding to the word covenant; on the other hand, where the *berith* lies between God and man, even though it possesses equally the character of a mutual agreement, they never employ συνθήκη but always διαθήκη. Plainly then their avoidance of the former is due to the thought that it connotes something that cannot be properly predicated of God. The preposition συν in συνθήκη expresses the co-equality and coëfficiency of the persons concerned in the *berith*. Such a coëquality and coëfficiency cannot exist between God and man; even where God most condescendingly enters upon a relation of true friendship with man, it is still out of place to conceive of this as a treaty in the ordinary sense. God cannot forego the right of sovereignly framing and imposing the arrangement that shall control the religious intercourse between Himself and man, and that He exercises this right is admirably expressed by the preposition διά in διαθήκη. To this extent and to this extent only we are warranted in saying that the

Septuagint shrinks from conceiving of the Old Testament religion as a "covenant." What it wants to avoid is the contractual character of the religious relation in its origin, not its reciprocal character in the outcome. The translators had no interest and could have no interest in representing God as the framer of a "last will" and the conveyor of property. All that they wanted out of *diatheke* was the emphasis which the word enabled them to throw upon the one-sided initiative and the unimpaired sovereignty of God in originating the order of redemption. And fortunately the linguistic usage did allow them to utilize the word for this purpose. Since the original etymological meaning of "a person's free disposition in his own interest" still clearly shows through the specialized sense of "testament", they could fall back upon it and were not compelled to take the technical associations of *diatheke* into the bargain. Had this been otherwise, had the word become so absolutely and irretrievably identified with the conception of a "last will", then the substitution of διαθήκη for συνθήκη in the sole interest of escaping from the synergistic, contractual implications of σύν would have been a desperate remedy. It would have meant for fear of misrepresenting the form to sacrifice the substance of the idea. Surely the Septuagint translators were not foolish enough to affirm, irrespective of all inevitable incongruities, that the *berith* was a "testament" simply because in one important respect they could not properly call it a "covenant". Their procedure appears intelligent only on the supposition that they believed *diatheke* capable of retaining or reacquiring the sense of "disposition". And it should be emphasized that in making *diatheke*, so understood, the vehicle for conveying the content of the Old Testament *berith* the Greek translators evince the most exquisite tact. The rendering represents not one of their blunders but one of their most felicitous strokes. The supreme interest they attach to safeguarding the divine dignity and prerogative is not something of later origin and imported by them ab extra into the Old Testament world of thought. On the contrary it constitutes one of the ideas indigenous to the Old Testament revelation itself. Thence and from no other source the Septuagint derived it. They prove themselves in this case excellent craftsmen by reason of their faculty of sympathetic apprehension no less than by reason of their skill in faithful reproduction. In one respect they even improved upon the Hebrew original: for, while in the Hebrew Scriptures the divine sovereignty in regulating the religious life of Israel is uniformly recognized and prevailingly colors the representation, it does not find direct expression in the word *berith* itself. Such expression the makers of the Greek Bible first gave it. They for the first time made the word and the conception cover each other with approximate perfection. And by thus enshrining the concept in the word, they created the means for the conservation and faithful transmission of a great religious treasure to the later Church.

We now approach the question, what data the New Testament passages offer for determining the sense of *diatheke*. Of course, the answers cannot help being strongly influenced by the conclusion reached regarding the Septuagint usage. Still we must not forget that the New Testament writers lived in a new-created world of redemptive realities and apprehended this world with new-born forms of thought. The possibility should be reckoned with that the ancient conception of the διαθήκη felt the effect of the powerful forces set free in the spheres of redemption and revelation. To what extent, we ask, do the facts show that such was actually the case? At the outset it may be well to moderate our expectation of fresh insight into the content of the idea to be afforded by the manner of its occurrence in the New Testament writings. As already stated, where it is not introduced in a purely retrospective sense but reinstated as a conception remaining permanently applicable to the new order of things ushered in by Christ, this is done largely in a comparative manner, that is to say, without much reflection upon the inherent character of the idea. The new order is a *diatheke* because the old order was. This is taken for granted rather than consciously realized through apprehension of the continuity of organic structure in both cases. Hence the difficulty of telling in many passages what conception the *diatheke* in such comparative statements actually called up to the writer's mind. It would be exegetically wrong to seek to elicit answers from such contexts on a question which probably was not present to the consciousness of the author at all. Still even so there are sufficient indications to enable us to affirm that the three senses, "covenant", "authoritative disposition", "testament", are all represented in the New Testament vocabulary. The idea of "covenant" in the specific sense, that is with positive reflection upon the community of interests, the intercourse and fellowship between God and man, is perhaps least in evidence. This does not necessarily mean that it was least familiar to the writers, only it so happens that it obtrudes itself less and its currency is therefore less easily verified. Outside of Hebrews the passages recording the institution of the Supper most clearly attest its presence. To be sure these are the very passages in which a number of modern expositors, Zahn, Deissmann, Dibelius, confidently claim that the meaning "testament" can be established with a strong degree of plausibility. Our Lord here brings the new *diatheke* into connection with the cup containing His blood, that is with His death. This invites the interpretation that through His death the new religious basis on which it puts His followers is as a legacy bequeathed to them. In favor of this view a further argument is drawn from Lk. 22:29, where, immediately after the institution of the Supper, our Lord speaks of the provision He makes for His followers in the future kingdom and uses to describe this act the word διατίθεσθαι, the rendering proposed being: "I bequeath unto you, as my Father bequeathed unto me etc." If the technical use of the verb could here be substantiated it would create a presumption in favor of the technical sense of the noun διαθήκη in the immediately preceding institution of the Supper, the more so since the imagery of joint-eating and -drinking with Jesus at His table on the one hand and the eschatological outlook of the Supper, in which Jesus also speaks of the drinking of new wine in the kingdom of God, on the other hand, appear to draw the two statements very closely together. These two arguments, weighty as they may seem at first sight, on closer inspection lose much of their force. It is true our Lord establishes a connection between His death and the new *diatheke* inaugurated. But this by no means shuts us up to viewing the *diatheke* as a testament put into effect through the death. The true interpretation of the Lord's Supper is that it appears as a sacrificial meal, to which His death forms the sacrifice. If, therefore, the new *diatheke* is connected with the death of Jesus, the connection will have to be sought along the line of sacrifice, that is to say, the death must be assumed to give birth to the *diatheke* in the same capacity and for the same reason which make it the central feature of the sacrament. It is, therefore, *à priori* probable that the *diatheke* appears as something inaugurated by a sacrifice, and that is not a "testament" but either a "religious disposition" or a "covenant". The obvious parallel in which Jesus places the blood of the new διαθήκη with that of Ex. 24, where the blood is none other than the blood of sacrifice inaugurating the Sinaitic *berith*, also requires this interpretation. And when it is said of the blood as exponential of the death that it is ὑπὲρ πολλῶν, "on behalf of many", this yields a thought utterly incongruous to the concept of testament, for a testator does not die in behalf of or with the intent of benefiting his heirs, whereas the benevolent intent of the death of a person fits admirably into the circle of sacrificial ideas. As to the passage from Luke, it is exceedingly doubtful whether the verb διατίθεσθαι can there have the technical meaning of "to bequeath" on which the force of the argument depends. Jesus, it will be observed, puts His own διατίθεσθαι for the disciples on a line with the Father's διατίθεσθαι for Himself. Now the Father's provision of the kingdom for Jesus, from the nature of the case, cannot be considered a testamentary act, since God does not die. This already compels the rendering: "I appoint unto you as my Father appointed unto me", with which we are familiar from our English Bible. To this must be added that the more plausible construction of the sentence makes the object of the διατίθεσθαι of Jesus for the disciples something that could hardly be the object of a testamentary disposition. The English versions construe: "I appoint unto you *a kingdom*, even as my Father appointed unto me a kingdom". But for reasons, which it is not necessary here to detail, the construction given by the Revised Version in the margin decidedly deserves the preference. It reads: "I appoint unto you that ye may eat and drink at my table in my kingdom, even as my Father *appointed* unto me a kingdom." If the object of Jesus' διατίθεσθαι for the disciples were a kingdom, as it is on the ordinary construction, this might properly fall under the rubric of a legacy, but the eating and drinking with a person in his kingdom do not naturally fall within the terms of a bequest. For these reasons we believe that the testamentary idea may safely be eliminated from the institution of the Lord's Supper. As to the choice between the two other meanings "disposition" and "covenant" the latter decidedly deserves the preference. The new *diatheke* appears from the point of view of its valuableness to the disciples. This already points to the covenant-idea. More specifically, the benefit conveyed by it consists in the approach to God mediated by the forgiveness of sins. It is equivalent to a new basis of intercourse between God and the disciples. Finally the pointed reference to the *berith* at Sinai, which was to all intents a two-sided agreement, and to the prophecy of Jeremiah, which speaks of the future new *berith* as a supreme favor to be bestowed upon Israel shows that the emphasis rests upon the resulting covenantal fellowship rather than upon the divine sovereign initiative that lies back of the new order of things.

A careful study of the Pauline passages yields a somewhat different result. It is true where Paul speaks retrospectively of the διαθῆκαι as forming part of the distinctions and prerogatives of Israel, as in Rom. 9:4 and Eph. 2:12, this might seem to favor the notion of "covenant" as involving a privileged relation to God. But in the passage of Romans the coordination of διαθῆκαι with such terms as "the promises" and "the law" proves that a one-sided disposition of God could easily be viewed as a favor and distinction conferred upon Israel. In Eph. 2:12 the phrase "covenants of the promise", in which the genitive is epexegetical, yields positive proof that Paul regards the διαθῆκαι as so many successive promissory dispositions of God, not as a series of mutual agreements between God and the people. Far more energetically however does the Pauline principle of the sole activity of God in the work of salvation draw the *diatheke*-idea into its service where the latter is considered not by manner of retrospect merely, but is applied on the comparative principle to the Christian system itself. Here every reflection on the covenantal aspect of the new religious relation is absent and the *diatheke*-idea is pointedly used to bring out how God sovereignly sets in motion and effectually organizes and carries through all that is necessary to securing the religious end contemplated in His purpose. Thus in 2 Corinthians 3 the two διαθῆκαι compared, that of the letter and that of the Spirit, represent two great systems and methods of religious procedure, working themselves out through two corresponding ministries, that of Moses and that of Paul, and thus inevitably shaping the result of human destiny and experience according to their intrinsic law of operation. The old *diatheke* is the system of legal administration: it issues into bondage, condemnation and death. The new *diatheke* is the system of spiritual procreation and endowment prevailing through Christ: it produces liberty, righteousness and life. The sense of contract is not only absent here: one may perhaps go so far as to say that the introduction of it would have jarred upon the singlemindedness wherewith the Apostle pursues the opposite element in the conception, that of the divine sovereignty and monergism of procedure. Only, over against Deissmann it should be observed that Paul pursues this principle in a thoroughly impartial way, with reference equally to the Old Dispensation, and to the New. In speaking of the order of grace as a *diatheke* in this one-sided divinely-monopolized sense, Paul is not conscious of imparting to the *diatheke* a different character from that which it bore previously. The legal order of things is as little a contract here as that which took its place: it was according to Paul a *diatheke* in the same absolute, sovereign way as the Gospel-order of things. The form is the same, the content poured into it differs; and the form as such is indifferent to the distinction between grace and works. Although there was an agreement at Sinai, in Paul's view it was evidently of such an origin and nature that it could be equally well represented as the result of a divine disposition and the name *diatheke* employed with exclusive reference to this its source in the activity of God.

The contrast between the Hagar-*diatheke* and the Sarah-*diatheke* in Galatians 4:24 proceeds along similar lines. That the Hagar-*diatheke* here stands for the old Sinaitic system, not in its original divine intent but in its Judaistic perversion, creates no formal difference; the *diatheke* is viewed here as in 2 Corinthians 3 as a project and organism determining religious status, bearing, propagating itself, as the figure strikingly expresses it, unto liberty as unto bondage.

The term is placed at the farthest remove from every association with "covenant" by Paul's way of handling it in Galatians 3. There can be little doubt that here the desire to throw the strongest possible emphasis on the supremacy of the principle of promise and grace in Old Testament history has induced the Apostle to compare the Abrahamic *diatheke* to a "testament". That Paul here has in mind a "testament" follows from two considerations: first, the legal terminology employed is derived from testamentary law and is such as was not used in connection with covenants or legal dispositions generally; second, in the context the idea of the *inheritance* is pointedly associated with the *diatheke*. The Apostle means to say, the gracious principle on which God pledged to Abraham and in him to all believers the inheritance of salvation was as absolutely immutable, as absolutely incapable of being modified or replaced by the subsequent law-giving, as if it had been a testamentary disposition: "A testament, though it be but a man's testament … no man makes void or adds thereto" … even so "a testament confirmed by God beforehand, the law which came four hundred and thirty years after doth not

disannul so as to make the promise of none effect." To our
minds it might easily seem as if the idea of a "testament"
were poorly adapted to bring out the character of
immutability which Paul wishes to emphasize. A "testament"
as we know it might more easily be a figure for
changeableness than the opposite, for until the testator dies
it is subject to repeated modification or absolute recall. How
then can Paul say: "*no one* maketh it void or addeth thereto."
It has been proposed to take "no one" in the sense of "no one
except the testator". But Paul evidently means "no one, not
even the testator", and the purpose for which he employs
the representation requires him to mean it so, for the point
is precisely this, that not even the testator, God, could
subsequently through the giving of the law have modified the
arrangement made with Abraham. It is plain, therefore, that
here is a "testament" which, once made, cannot be changed.
Professor Ramsay, I believe, has furnished the solution to
this difficulty by calling attention to the difference between
the testament of Roman law and a kind of testament possible
under Syro-Grecian law.[3] The Roman testament, as we
know it, is changeable till the testator dies, but under the
Syro-Grecian law a prospective disposition of property
could be made during the lifetime of the possessor,
frequently carrying with it adoption, which after having
been once sanctioned in public immediately carried with it

---

[3] *Expositor,* 1899, pp. 57 ff.

certain effects and was not after that subject to modification. Comparing the *berith* God made with Abraham to such a *diatheke* Paul could within the terms of the representation properly say that God could not have meant to change its fundamental character as a dispensation of grace and promise through the later giving of the law at Sinai, and that therefore the law may not be interpreted on a legalistic principle but must be subsumed under the Abrahamic arrangement as a means to an end. Perhaps it will be said that Paul by giving this turn to the *diatheke* has imported into it what the *berith*-idea of Gen. 15 did not contain, in other words, that in saying God meant it so when making the promise to Abraham, the Apostle is historically at fault. The charge would be warranted, of course, if Paul had used this peculiar testamentary conception for a different purpose than that for which in Genesis the *berith*-idea is introduced. But this is by no means the case. The purpose for which in the one case the form of the *berith*, in the other case that of the "testament" comes in, is absolutely identical. The *berith* with Abraham was not a covenantal *berith* at all. It was a disposition-*berith* in the strictest sense, intended exclusively by God for the purpose of binding Himself in the strongest possible way by His own promise, and so rendering the promise unalterably sure. It is for nothing else than for faithfully translating this import of the *berith* into the thought-form of his readers and so bringing it home to their understanding that Paul says God made with Abraham a testamental *diatheke*. Under the circumstances this amounted to saying: the *berith* God made with Abraham was as unchangeable as a *diatheke* is among you. It simply accentuates, in the most emphatic way, what to the narrator of Genesis himself is the salient point of the transaction.

Before returning to Hebrews, we must cast a glance at the use of the conception in the two cases where Luke records it. In the Gospel 1:72 the *diatheke* is equivalent to the promise given to the fathers; the parallelism in which it stands with the "oath" of God proves this: "to remember his holy *diatheke*, the oath which He swore unto Abraham, our father." In the other passage, Acts 3:25, Peter addresses the Jews as "sons of the prophets" and "sons of the *diatheke* which God made with the fathers". "Sons of the prophets" of course does not mean "descendants of the prophets" but "heirs of what the prophets have predicted". Similarly "sons of the *diatheke* does not mean "begotten by the *diatheke*", but "heirs of what the *diatheke* conveys in the way of blessing". This, of course, admits, though it by no means positively requires the construction of the *diatheke* as a "testament". "Heirs of a testament-*diatheke*" is a more suggestive, and more directly self-explanatory form of statement than "heirs of a disposition-*diatheke*". But it can not be said that the latter interpretation is in itself unnatural. "Sons of the *berith*" for "heirs of the promise of the *berith*" is as allowable a figure, as good Semitic idiom, as "sons of the prophets" for "heirs of the predictions of the prophets". But, whether the notion of "testament" be found here or not, it is at any rate clear that

the Lucan and Petrine usage in these two passages agrees
with the prevailing Pauline mode of representation. Peter,
like Paul, emphasizes the sovereign promissory source of
God's dealings with His people and does not reflect in the
present connection upon the reciprocal relation resulting
from it. In passing it may be remarked that in Stephen's
speech, Acts 7:8, "the *diatheke* of circumcision" means
nothing else but "the law, ordinance of circumcision". The
reference is to Gen. 17, where the word *berith* has the same
sense. The author of Genesis, who in chapter 15 used the
term *berith* in the sense of a promise, here takes it as "law",
"appointment". He did not mean that God in the same sense
twice made a *berith* with the patriarch. First God gave a
promise-*berith*, then He imposed a law-*berith*. So Genesis
intends it and so Stephen quotes it.

We are now ready to return to Hebrews and bring to
bear upon it the light we have obtained from the remainder
of the New Testament. In view of what has been found, it is
not likely that *diatheke* bears in the Epistle the uniform
meaning of "testament". Riggenbach's assertion to this effect
is staked on the fact that in 9:16, 17 the necessity of
rendering "testament" is self-evident, and that this one
passage must be considered regulative for the author's
understanding of the term throughout. The major premise
of this argument is unassailable. The wording of the
statement in the passage named compels us to think of a
testament: "where a *diatheke* is, there must of necessity be

the death of him that made it, for a *diatheke* is of force where there has occurred death: for does it ever avail while he that made it liveth?" Besides this, the purposeful introduction of technical law-terms is just as noticeable here as in Galatians 3. Of course there have been exegetes who thought they could even here adhere to the meaning "covenant". Westcott is one of these.[4] He thinks that the necessity of death dwelt upon in the passage has nothing to do with the legal decease of a testator, but relates to sacrificial death. According to him the thought is: a covenant cannot go into effect except a sacrificial victim have died. It does not, of course, escape Westcott that the author, instead of saying this, makes the quite different assertion, a covenant cannot go into effect except the *covenant-maker* have died. How can that possibly be explained on the principle of sacrifice? Westcott appeals for explaining it to the idea of identification between the offerer and his sacrifice, so that when the animal dies the offerer, in this case the covenant-maker, dies with it. "He who makes a covenant is, for the purposes of the covenant, identified with the sacrificial victim, by whose representative death the covenant is ordinarily ratified. In the death of the victim his death is presented symbolically." In other words the author of Hebrews meant really to say: "A covenant cannot go into effect except in his sacrificial substitute the covenant-maker has first died." There can be no objection to the symbolical-vicarious interpretation of sacrifice in general

---

[4] The Epistle to the Hebrews, p. 265.

or of covenant-sacrifice in particular. We believe most thoroughly in its soundness. But that does not answer the question why the author of Hebrews should in this passage have found it necessary to call attention to the fact that not merely the sacrifice but in the sacrifice the covenant-maker dies, and that only so the covenant can go into effect. Westcott himself feels the necessity of accounting for this peculiar form of statement, and therefore offers the additional explanation that the death of the covenant-maker in the sacrifice serves to express the idea of the subsequent unchangeableness of the covenant: "the unchangeableness of the covenant is seen in the fact that he who has made it has deprived himself of all further power of movement in this respect." The man is dead and can no longer act. On the impossibility of this explanation the whole exegesis breaks down. The idea of unchangeableness, irrevocableness of the covenant, on which Westcott would suspend it, is foreign to the context. What the writer wants to prove by the death of Christ is not the subsequent unchangeableness or irrevocableness of the *diatheke* but its sure effectuation. Herein lies precisely the difference between Gal. 3 and this 9 chapter of Hebrews. Paul says no one *annuls* or *adds* thereunto; our author says: a *diatheke avails, is of force, goes into effect* when a person dies. Besides this, if the writer had actually wanted to express the thought of irrevocableness and unchangeableness, the representation of the *diatheke* as a testament in the Roman-law-sense would have lain far nearer to his hand and be far more suited to his purpose, than this tortuous, artificial appeal to symbolic suicide of the covenant-maker in his sacrifice. Still further, the full absurdity of the exegesis is felt only when the attempt is made to apply the principle in question to the death of Jesus. Can we say that the covenant inaugurated by Jesus through the sacrifice of Himself is now irrevocable and unchangeable because, the covenant-maker now being dead, the covenant is ipso facto exempted from all danger of change or annulment? The case of Jesus is precisely peculiar in this, that He does not remain dead; the whole ingenious device of proving the unchangeableness from the death would be a mere pretense at argument, lacking all cogency for the case in hand. We may, therefore, confidently dismiss this exegesis as impossible. The *diatheke* in Heb. 9:16, 17 is nothing else but a "testament", and its testamentary aspect serves the single purpose of bringing out the certainty of its effectuation. Just as the death of a testator under the Roman law automatically puts into effect his last will, even so the death of Christ with absolute inevitability secures all the effects for which it was intended.

Now, Riggenbach's major premise being thus granted, are we bound to accept his conclusion, that *diatheke* must uniformly throughout the Epistle mean the same thing that it means here? We think not. There are several considerations that lead us to believe that the treatment of the *diatheke* as a "testament" is a peculiarity of this one passage and not representative of the author's ordinary view. The very fact that the author takes great pains by the use of legal terminology to call the reader's attention to the possibility of construing the *diatheke* as a "testament" operates against the view that it should ordinarily have been so understood either by him or by the readers. Then there is the important phenomenon that the author immediately before and after the passage under discussion predicates things of the *diatheke* which do not properly belong to a "testament". In verse 15 the death of Christ is said to have taken place for the redemption from transgressions committed under a former *diatheke*. "Transgressions" do not naturally invalidate a "testament", but do have a disannulling effect upon a "covenant" or a "disposition." And in verse 18 the writer says: "Wherefore even the first *diatheke* has not been *dedicated* without blood". It is plain that here already the idea of "testament" has been again dismissed as suddenly as it had been introduced; the author has shifted back to his ordinary conception of the *diatheke* as a "covenant" or a "disposition", for to a "testament" the idea of "dedication" does not apply. Evidently the writer finds it difficult to keep himself well within the terms of the figurative, accommodating use to which for the moment he is led to put the conception. Finally it is still possible to point out what it was that first suggested to the author the rendering "testament" as a means of which he might avail himself to set forth impressively the effectiveness of the death of Christ. This was nothing else than the mention of "the inheritance" at the close of verse 15: "For this cause is He the mediator of a new *diatheke* that a death having taken place for the redemption from the transgressions that were under the first *diatheke*, they who have been called may receive the promise of the eternal inheritance." The author in speaking of the inheritance is at first still unconscious of the train of thought which it may open up. But no sooner has he written down the word than all at once the possibility of attaching the inheritance to the *diatheke* in the sense of "testament" suggests itself to him and he is quick to see the striking use that may be made of it in furtherance of his argument. But the novel turn given to the word under such circumstances offers no indication of the meaning connected with it elsewhere in the Epistle. To assume that it signifies "testament" elsewhere we need other evidence than this single passage. And such evidence does not exist. In none of the other contexts where *diatheke* occurs is there anything that even remotely suggests the idea of a last will. And against it speaks decisively the representation of Jesus as the sponsor and mediator of the new *diatheke*. Neither of these two functions that of a sponsor or that of a mediator appear among the legal accompaniments of a testament.

But if not the idea of a testament, what then is the idea which our Epistle ordinarily connects with the word *diatheke*? The answer is that both the other aspects of the conception so far found in the earlier documents are here represented with a fair degree of equilibrium. The usage of our Lord, who spoke of a "new covenant", and that of Paul, who practically everywhere views the *diatheke* as a divine disposition, both reappear in Hebrews, and they are not merely mechanically held together but organically and harmoniously united. The Epistle speaks the last word in the Biblical development of the *berith-diatheke* idea and that not only in point of chronology but likewise as giving the idea its full-orbed, consummate expression. And this is due to the fact previously alluded to, that the writer of Hebrews is positively interested in the conception, loves it for its own inherent character, finds it congenial to his own religious idiosyncrasy, and so is able to penetrate it with his thought and raise it to the highest state of doctrinal fruitfulness. The two aspects distinguishable in the *diatheke* correspond closely to the two poles between which the religious thinking of the author moves. His thinking would have partaken of this twofold character even if the *diatheke*-idea had remained unknown to him; the latter is by no means the source of his doctrine but, as a reagent, it has materially contributed to the strengthening and clarifying of the two great thoughts that existed and worked in the writer's mind apart from it. Let us look at each of these two thoughts separately and at the corresponding elements in the *diatheke* with which they are found interacting.

In studying the Epistle it soon becomes clear that it deals with the *diatheke* from two different points of view. In a number of passages it appears as an institution established and set in operation for an ulterior end. This is in line with the understanding of the *diatheke* as a divine disposition, and leaves out of regard its character as a state of fellowship with God, in which latter respect it is not, of course, a means to an end, but an absolute end in itself. It is true the direction to an ulterior purpose admits of being combined with the idea of a covenant: a covenant between two parties can serve to realize some extrinsic end. As a matter of fact, however, while this may be so in the abstract, the concrete statements of the Epistle in regard to the ends which the *diatheke* subserves are such as to exclude the idea of their being reached by a "covenant" and fit in only with the idea of a system or disposition. The instrumental *diatheke* appears in the following ways. Back of the *diatheke* stand the promises, and it is for the fulfillment of the promises that the *diatheke* has been instituted. Hence it is said to have been enacted upon the basis of promises, inferior promises in the case of the first *diatheke*, better ones in the case of the second. The *diatheke* further appears as a means to the end of the τελείωσις, *i.e.* the attainment of the religious goal of approach to and communion with and service of God. Here, it will be seen, the fellowship with God, which we ordinarily associate with the covenant-idea appears as lying above and beyond the *diatheke*, as the end lies above and beyond the means.

Over against this we may place other passages in the Epistle which represent the *diatheke* as the realisation of the religious ideal and therefore as an end in itself. In 8:10, in the passage quoted from Jeremiah, the *diatheke* is held to consist in this, that Jehovah is the God of Israel, and Israel to Jehovah a people. The life of the people of God is essentially an intercourse with God and this intercourse appears in 9:14, 15 as the very essence of the *diatheke*. The *diatheke* is also called a διαθήκη αἰώνιος, "an everlasting covenant", chap. 13:20, and this implies that in it the whole religious process comes to rest: for the predicate αἰώνιος in Hebrews expresses not only endless duration but inclusion among the eternal realities which have absolute value and significance in themselves. Now it is plain that in this second absolute aspect the character of the *diatheke* can only be expressed by the rendering "covenant". It is only as a "covenant" and not as a disposition that it lends itself to being eternalized after this fashion.

These two principal aspects of the *diatheke* answer perfectly to the two outstanding features of the Epistle's teaching. The first of these consists in the emphasis placed upon the absoluteness, sovereignty and majesty of God and the monergistic divine initiative and prosecution of the work of salvation. In various ways, altogether apart from the *diatheke*-conception, this finds expression. God is the Majesty on high (1:3), the one for whom are all things and through whom are all things, whom it therefore behooves, even through great suffering with sovereign hand to carry through His saving purpose (2:10), the living God (9:15, 11:31), a consuming fire (12:29). But in keeping with this the writer vindicates for God not merely the original planning and inception but also the further effectual carrying out of the work of redemption. There are various servants in the house of God, and Christ is even a son over the house, but the principle remains in force: "He that built all things is God" (3:5). And how this thought of the underlying divine initiative and energizing flows together with the *diatheke*-idea may be seen from the doxology in 13:20, 21: it is the God who omnipotently brought again from the dead the Lord Jesus, with the blood of the eternal *diatheke*, who also makes the believers perfect in every good thing to do His will, working in them that which is well-pleasing in His sight through Jesus Christ. On this principle it is further to be explained that the new *diatheke* can be represented as a new species of legislation. God has enacted it. The reason is not that it is legalistic in content or import, but simply that God has instituted it with the same supreme authority with which He promulgates His law. How much weight the author attaches to this point may be seen from the change introduced in 9:20 into the quotation from Ex. 24:8. Here the Septuagint reads: "this is the blood of the *diatheke* which God *disposed* (διέθετο) towards you". The writer substitutes for this: "the blood of the *diatheke* which God *commanded* towards you." In line with this conception of the *diatheke* as a divine arrangement carrying the pledge of its unfailing effectuation in itself is also the function of ἱεμστης and ἔγγυος performed by Christ in connection with it. Of the latter term ἔγγυος, to be rendered as "sponsor", this is plain on the surface. Christ is the "sponsor" of the *diatheke* insofar as He guarantees the fulfilment of the promises to which the *diatheke* has reference. The term is not a technical term either in connection with a "testament" or a "covenant" and it most naturally attaches itself to the understanding of *diatheke* as a divine promissory dispensation. It forms the connecting link between the *diatheke* and the important rôle which the word "promise", "promises", plays in the Epistle. As for μεσίτης, the English literal rending of the word by "mediator" is apt to lead to the premature conclusion that it goes with the *diatheke* as a two-sided covenantal agreement and marks Jesus as the one who brings the two parties together by mediating between them. While μεσίτης has this meaning in the Greek language of law, its legal use is by no means restricted to it and at least three other meanings have been fully established as equally current.[5] We shall not weary the reader with an account of the recent discussions on this point: suffice it to say that the trend of present scholarship is towards considering μεσίτης and ἔγγυος as entirely synonymous in the vocabulary of the writer of Hebrews. The μεσίτης is he who guarantees for God the

---

[5] The other three meanings are: 1) the person with whom parties at law deposit the object in litigation until the suit has been decided; 2) the witness who vouches for the veracity of a statement; in this sense the verb μεσιτεύειν is used in chap. 6:17 God pledged Himself with an oath for the truthfulness of His promise; 3) the person who vouches for the execution of engagements made; in this sense μεσίτης becomes synonymous with ἔγγυος.

sure accomplishment of what has been stated or promised in the διαθήκη. So taken the word, no less than ἔγγυος, becomes a witness to the prominence in the writer's mind of the sovereign, promissory aspect of the *diatheke*.

The other aspect of the *diatheke*, that of covenantal fellowship and intercourse with God appealed equally much, if not more, to the religious temperament of the writer. It has long been observed that the type of Christianity represented by the Epistle is peculiar in the almost exclusive emphasis it places upon the exercise of religion in the conscious sphere. The important subconscious processes, sometimes designated as mystical, which play so large a role in the Pauline teaching, are very little in evidence in Hebrews. Hence also the Spirit as the author and bearer of this hidden subconscious union with God and Christ is seldom referred to. Where the Holy Spirit is mentioned in Hebrews it is as the source of the extraordinary charismata, and even here His operation is highly personal, for He is said to distribute these gifts according to His own will (2:4). It would be foolish, of course, to attribute the absence of this specifically Pauline strand of teaching to the author's ignorance or denial of it. The many and intimate relations with Paul's type of doctrine in other respects forbid us to assume any conscious departure or opposition here. But without ignoring or denying the deeper and more mysterious underground of the religious process, the author could feel himself more strongly drawn towards exploring and cultivating the more advanced stage of the process, for whose sake all previous operations exist, its blossoming out into conscious Christian experience. The author of Hebrews is a great spiritualizer. The efflorescence of religion in the clear luminous regions of the believer's noëtic life evokes his supreme interest. In several important connections we can trace the influence of this spiritualizing factor in the shaping of his thought. These will afterwards receive separate attention. For the present it suffices to observe that to a mind thus spiritually oriented the interpretation of religion in terms of the covenant was bound to offer a special attraction. For it is precisely in religion as a covenant-religion that everything is reduced to ultimate, spiritual, conscious values. The new covenant is the ideal covenant because in it the will and law of God are internalized, put on the heart and written upon the mind. Here its nature as a covenant can first freely and perfectly unfold itself.

The full significance, however, of this interlocking of the principle of spirituality in religion and the covenant-idea will not be perceived until we remember in the next place that the spiritualizing tendency of the Epistle is of a peculiar, God-centered kind, and that only in this specific form it perfectly fits into the covenant-type of religion. We do not hesitate to say that in hardly any New Testament writing is the essential character of the Christian religion as consisting in face to face intercourse with God, mediated by Jesus Christ, so clearly realized and so pointedly brought out as in our Epistle. The supremacy of the spiritual, when closely looked at, is only a result of drawing every religious state and act into the immediate presence of God, where nothing but the spiritual can abide. To be a Christian is to live one's life not merely in obedience to God, nor merely in dependence on God, nor even merely for the sake of God; it is to stand in conscious, reciprocal fellowship with God, to be identified with Him in thought and purpose and work, to receive from Him and give back to Him in the ceaseless interplay of spiritual forces. It is this direct confrontation of the religious mind with God which finds in the covenant-idea its perfect expression. To be in covenant with God,— what finer and what more adequate definition of the perfect religious life could be conceived than this? The classical formula in which already under the Old Testament God Himself expresses His conception of the covenant and which through Jeremiah has descended to our author reads: "I shall be to them a God and they shall be to me a people", and "All shall know me from the least to the greatest." According to this the covenant means that God gives Himself to man and man gives Himself to God for that full measure of mutual acquaintance and enjoyment of which each side to the relation is capable. The highest concrete analogy for this is that offered by the prophet Hosea when he compares the *berith* between Jehovah and the people to the marriage-bond between husband and wife, which when perfect leaves no room for divided interests or possessions. Some of the Psalms also reach the same high altitude where the soul rises above every thought of self, even above the consciousness of its own need of salvation, and desires and receives God for His own sake.

Let us now endeavor to trace the influence which this covenantal understanding of the relation between God and man has exerted upon the theology of the Epistle. And first of all its doctrine of revelation must be considered here. The Epistle makes much of the fact that God has revealed Himself to His people. In part, of course, this is accounted for by the supernaturalism which the writer has in common with all the Biblical writers. No redemptive religion, however conceived, covenantal or otherwise, can dispense with the basis of divine, supernatural self-disclosure. But there are perceptible differences in the way in which the several types of Biblical teaching account for this necessity and in the statement of the supreme end which they make it subserve. Special, supernatural revelation is necessary for a soteriological reason, because man in his sinful, lost, helpless condition is dependent on the sovereign, gracious approach of God in word and act to recover his normal religious state. As such, revelation bears an instrumental saving character. This view of it also Hebrews shares with the other New Testament writings. Revelation, however, alongside of this, and even through all its saving activity also serves the purpose of establishing as from God to man that train of personal communication in which the end of religion consists. In this aspect one might define it as divine speech for the sake of divine speech; God reveals Himself, because in His love for His own and interest in them it is natural for Him to open up and communicate Himself. Revelation in a sense is the highest that God has to give because in it He gives Himself. And while in the ordinary understanding of it revelation is in order to salvation, the reversed sequence also can lay claim to recognition: salvation is in order to prepare man for further, perpetual revelation carrying its right of existence in itself. Such speech of God existed in the state of rectitude; such will continue to exist in the eschatological state of the world to come, when all abnormality of sin and every need of salvation shall have been forever surmounted. And, as already intimated, even in the soteric process of revelation this higher and ultimate function of it finds simultaneous employment. All saving transactions are so many approaches, so many occasions of meeting between God and man in which the forces of help become fountains of love, God the great physician of souls making friends of all His patients. Now it is in the emphasis placed upon this specifically religious aspect of revelation that the influence of the covenant-idea can be clearly traced in our Epistle. It is not accidental, that the first sentence with which the writer opens his discourse reads: "God having spoken … spake." It is as a speaking God that he grasps Him and desires to bring Him in touch with the readers. And the word also that is employed in this first sentence and prevailingly afterwards to describe the revelation-speech of God deserves notice in this connection. It is the verb λαλεῖν, a verb used in the New Testament with reference to the speech of God outside of Hebrews only in John and Acts and which brings out most strikingly the idea of familiar intercourse, denoting speech not primarily for the purpose of conveying information but for the purpose of maintaining fellowship. Further the verb διαλέγεσθαι, expressive of the two-sided mutually responsive speech that takes place between God and man may here be mentioned as entering into the author's vocabulary. Because the divine word is not merely for instruction or salvation but brings God personally near to the believer, it becomes in itself an object of enjoyment, hence the Epistle speaks of tasting the good word of God (6:5). And it is further in agreement with this personal, practical view taken of revelation when, throughout, the direct provenience of the word from God is emphasized. In a very striking way God regularly appears as the speaking subject in the quotations made from the Old Testament. Where Paul contents himself with the formula, "as it is written", or "as the Scripture says", Hebrews prefers to make the affirmation of the divine authorship explicit and employs the formula "God says". That this is not the result of meaningless habit, but possesses doctrinal significance, appears from the cases, where, rhetorically considered, it would be unnatural to introduce God as the speaking subject, since in the passage quoted He is the Person spoken of. Even in such cases the author insists upon emphasizing that the statement about God came from the mouth of God Himself. It is God who said "the Lord shall judge His people (10:30). And so vivid is the realisation of this supreme fact of the direct divine authorship of Scripture that what we call the secondary authors, that is, the writers of the Biblical books, are, again in distinction from Paul's custom, scarcely ever mentioned. The only case where the name of a Bible writer is introduced is chap. 4:7, and even here the phrase is not "David saying" but "God saying in David." There are even passages where pains seem to have been taken to bring out the relative unimportance of the secondary authorship by more positive means than the mere omission of the writer's name. In a couple of instances use seems to have been made for this purpose of the indefinite pronoun "some one" and the indefinite adverb "somewhere": "*One* has *somewhere* testified saying" (2:6); "For He hath spoken *somewhere* of the seventh day on this wise" (4:4). By this manner of statement the impression is conveyed that in view of the authority wherewith God invests every word of Scripture the human instrumentality through which the divine word was mediated becomes a matter of little or no importance. As a matter of fact the word of revelation is so literally to the writer's mind the word of God that it is represented as having been spoken by God being locally present in His messengers: "God of old times spoke unto the fathers *in* the prophets"; "God said *in* David". The conception is not instrumental, as if "in" were a Hebraizing construction for "by means of"; it should rather be compared with the similar form of statement by our Lord to the disciples: "it is not ye that speak, but the Spirit of your Father that speaketh in you" (Mat. 10:20), and by Paul who offers to the Corinthians a proof of Christ speaking in him (2 Cor. 13:3).

But, while this immediateness of the approach of God to man through His word is made a characteristic of all revelation, and found illustrated in the Old Testament Scriptures, the writer evidently associates it in the highest degree with the New Covenant. Over against the many portions and the many modes in which the ancient speech of God came to the people in the several prophets, he places that uniform and undivided revelation that was concentrated in Him who is a Son. The purpose for which the author draws this contrast is precisely to exalt the New Covenant by reason of the absolutely unmediated and most intimate union with man upon which in it through Christ God's revelation-speech has entered. Revelation in a Son is superior to that in prophets and superior to that in angels because as Son of God Christ is the effulgence of the divine glory and the expressed image of the divine substance, in no wise differing from God Himself, so that to hear His voice is to hear in the most literal sense God's own voice and to come in direct touch with the divine life expressing itself in the divine word. It is characteristic of the Epistle that, in connection with the revealing office of Christ, it places all the stress upon His divine nature, whereas in connection with His priestly office, the reality of His human nature is strongly emphasized. Both features are explainable from the covenant-idea. In regard to the priestly function we shall have occasion to show this later on. At this point it may be observed that the ideal revelation, if it is to fulfill its covenant-purpose of establishing real contact between God and man, can have no other than a strictly divine Mediator. Otherwise the bearer of the divine word would intervene between the covenant-God and the covenant-people and stand as a barrier to the close union contemplated. The perfect identification of Christ with God, therefore, is necessary to the belief that the Son has brought the highest and final revelation and raised the covenant-intercourse to a point beyond which it cannot be perfected. This can be observed most clearly perhaps on the negative side. Repeatedly the readers are warned in the Epistle that unbelief over against the New Testament revelation and rejection of its Gospel are a far more serious offense and must be followed by far more tremendous consequences than a similar line of conduct under the old dispensation. "Therefore we ought to give the more earnest heed to the things that were heard, lest haply we drift away. For if the word spoken through angels proved steadfast and every transgression and disobedience received a just recompense of reward; how shall we escape, if we neglect so great salvation (2:1–3)?" And "A man that hath set at naught Moses' law dieth without compassion on the testimony of two or three witnesses: of how much sorer punishment, think ye, shall he be judged worthy, who hath trodden under foot the Son of God, and hath counted the blood of the covenant, wherewith He was sanctified, an unholy thing, and hath done despite unto the Spirit of grace" (10:28–30)? "See that ye refuse not Him that speaketh. For if they escaped not when they refused Him that gave oracles on earth, much more shall not we escape, if we turn away from Him that gives oracles from Heaven" (12:25, 26). In such passages the revelation mediated by angels and by Moses and by the prophets is represented as imposing a lesser degree of responsibility than that mediated by Christ. Now the reason for this cannot lie in the fact that the angelic or Mosaic or prophetic message was insufficiently authenticated as to its divine origin or less completely derived from God. On the contrary the author explicitly states that the word spoken through angels proved steadfast, βέβαιος, and the same thing is emphasized regarding the Mosaic revelation at Sinai: neither of these could be disobeyed with impunity. But neither of these two, nor even the prophetic word, could be placed on a line with the revelation in Christ because here the word spoken comes invested with the divine majesty which it derives from the unique organ of its transmission, the Son of God. The measure of responsibility here evidently is not the truthfulness of the message, for that is alike in all true revelation, but the closeness of contact with God that is effected. Under the Old Testament there was not that immediateness and directness which the author claims for the self-disclosure of God in Christ. Between God and the people there stood the angels and Moses; between God and us stands only the Son. And, strictly speaking, even this is an incorrect form of statement which fails to reproduce the author's intent at its most vital point: as regards Christ, no intervention between God and us in the matter of revelation can be affirmed. By Christ's activity in this sphere absolutely nothing is detracted from the immediacy of the divine approach to man. Hence "the word of Christ" (6:1) is spoken of in precisely the same sense as is ordinarily connected with "the word of God", and in which "the word of Moses" or "the word of the prophets" could never be referred to. A stronger proof of the author's belief in the deity of our Lord than this whole representation that God spake under the Old Covenant through intermediate organs but under the New Covenant in Christ directly cannot be conceived.

But the practical character of revelation as a covenant-speech shows itself in still another way. The Epistle conceives of the divine word as not merely proceeding from God originally, but as also remaining in living contact with God ever afterwards. God continues to stand back of His revelation, nay abides immanent in it. The Scriptures of the Old Testament and the word spoken in Christ are as personal an address from God to the later generations as they were to those who first heard the divine voice proclaim them. The author is at the farthest remove from considering

the word by itself as a detached deposit of truth separated
from the mind that conceived or the mouth that spoke it,
having its own objective existence. It is significant that all his
statements on this subject refer to revelation in terms of
speech and not in terms of writing. The speech is an organic,
living process, a part and function of the speaking person,
whereas the written communication is only a picture or
symbol of the life-process it reproduces. But God's word,
even when written, has this peculiarity that it retains the
character of inspired, vitalized speech, opening up the
depths of the divine mind and addressing itself in the most
direct face-to-face way to the inner personality of the
hearer. So vividly does the author realize this, that in a well-
known passage it leads him to a formal personification of the
λόγος τοῦ θεοῦ in which attributes and activities are
predicted of the word, belonging, strictly speaking, to God
Himself only, and in which a remarkable transition is made
from the word to God as coordinate subjects in the same
sentence: "The word of God is living and active and sharper
than any two-edged sword, and piercing even to the dividing
of soul and spirit, both in their joints and marrow, and quick
to discern the thoughts and intents of the heart. And there is
no creature that is not manifest in *His* sight; but all things are
naked and open before the eyes of *Him* with whom we have
to do" (4:12–14). Misled by the vividness of the
personification some have thought that the author here
speaks of Christ as the personal Logos after the manner of

the Johannine teaching. But of the Logos-Christ it would have been unnecessary to affirm with such pointed emphasis that in His operation He is living and active and incisive, because His personality is self-evident, and what the writer by means of these predicates here wants to affirm of the word of God is nothing else than that it works as a personal agent upon the soul of man as a personal reagent. God acts in and through His word and thus the word has the same power and effect that belong to God Himself. Especially the figure of the sword searching the vitals and laying bare the inner attitude and disposition of man is very striking. Because the word of God confronts man with God personally he cannot in the presence of it remain neutral and treat it after an indifferent, disinterested fashion; it is a challenge to his soul that must provoke reaction and incite to faith or unbelief according to the inner disposition of the heart with reference to God.

Owing to this permanent identification of God with His word, the lapse of time is not able to detract aught from the freshness and force that belonged to the self-disclosure of God at its first historic occurrence. It is not necessary to project one's self backward through the interval of the ages in order to feel near to the source of the revelation. The fountain of the living water flows close to every believer. The author might have said with Moses and Paul: "Say not who shall ascend into heaven, or who shall descend into the abyss? The word is nigh thee, in thy mouth and in thy heart:

such is the word of faith which we preach" (Rom. 10:6–8; Deut. 30:12–14). It is true, the Epistle speaks not only of the καινή but also of the νέα διαθήκη and the latter phrase represents the new covenant as fresh and recent in comparison with the more remote Mosaic revelation. It should, however, be observed that, although the Epistle is addressed to Christians of the second generation, it none the less conceives of its readers as in the most immediate sense made recipients of the divine word spoken by Christ and through that word brought into no less direct communion with the supernatural world than the cotemporaries of the earthly life of Jesus. God spake unto the fathers in the prophets: He spake in a Son unto *us*. And through this speech they have come unto Mount Zion, and unto the city of the living God, nay unto God and Jesus the mediator of a fresh covenant Himself and, as we have seen, the danger incurred by disregarding this speech of God in Christ is for them no less but greater than it was for those who refused a hearing to the terrible voice of the Sinaitic legislation. The word remains what it was at the beginning when it fell fresh from the lips of Christ, a signal of the presence of God and a vehicle of approach for the world of the supernatural.

Part 2

Originally published in *The Princeton Theological Review*, 1916.

So far we have considered the Epistle's idea of revelation only from the practical point of view.[6] It has, however, a more theoretical side and this also shows the influence of the covenant-conception. More than any other New Testament document Hebrews develops what might be called a philosophy of the history of revelation. This is partly due to the fact that the writer is theologically inclined in general, and evidently attaches importance to the doctrinal presentation of the Christian faith. It would be a mistake to explain this from speculative tendencies followed for their own sake. Of a purely scholastic interest there is no trace whatever. But the writer entertains a firm belief in the effectiveness of doctrinal enlightenment as a remedial method where the soundness and balance of practical Christianity are endangered. We certainly gain the impression that from the outset he brings to the writing of the Epistle a well-defined doctrinal conception of the structure of the Christian religion. It can cause no wonder that, when a mind of this cast is led to occupy itself with the history of revelation, as is actually the case in our Epistle, a more or less philosophical or theological construction of the history of revelation results. We should, moreover, remember, that from the very earliest times the covenant-idea stood not merely in the service of revealed religion in general, but had also lent itself to the very particular use of marking the historic progress of the movement of

____

[6] In this Review, 1915 (xiii), pp. 587–632.

redemption and special revelation. The successive stages of God's redemptive and revealing work in the pre-Christian era are measured by successive covenants, each introducing new forces and principles and each imparting to the ensuing period a distinctive character of its own. Thus the covenant-idea is an eminently historical idea, most intimately associated with the gradual unfolding of God's self-disclosure to His people. This reaches even back of the régime of redemption and characterizes God's dealings with man in the state of rectitude. For, although it is generally considered a dogmatic anachronism to carry the covenant-idea back into the original religious status of unfallen man, as the Reformed Theology has done in its doctrine of the covenant of works, a most striking confirmation of the biblical warrant for this view has of late come from an altogether unexpected quarter. No less a scholar than Wellhausen has observed that in P, the so-called priestly document, the ancient history is represented as determined in its onward movement by the four covenants which in succession God makes with man, whence also the name of "the four-covenant-book" has come into use to designate the peculiar structure of this document. And as the first of these four covenants, it is maintained by Wellhausen and others, the author must have counted the arrangement entered into by God with our first parents in their original state. Thus the much ridiculed "covenant of works" has been exegetically rehabilitated and it has been shown that the Reformed theologians were not so utterly lacking in historic sense as their critics believed. In regard to the redemptive developments recorded in the Old Testament, it is plain that these result in large measure from the repeated and progressive subsumption of the people of God under the principle of the *berith*. With the critical contention that this is a later dogma first introduced into the older documents by the redactors we need not here occupy ourselves, since the writer of Hebrews could reckon and did reckon only with the Old Testament in its present form, in which the influence of the *berith*-idea is confessedly present. The comparative tenor of the Epistle would therefore of itself invite the representation of this idea as one of the chief factors in the development of sacred history. But the actual extent to which this is done by the writer is due to still another more specific cause. The Epistle does not content itself with dividing the history of redemption and revelation into two διαθῆκαι from a purely soteriological point of view: it brings the covenant-idea into connection with eschatology and by doing this first introduces into it the breadth and absoluteness that pertain to the eschatological outlook. So long as the consciousness of redemption contents itself with living in the present moment, or ranges over a limited outlook backwards and forwards, the theological impulse may remain dormant and no desire need be felt to bring order and system into the wealth of the divine acts and disclosures as one after the other they enter into the cognition or experience of man. But the matter becomes entirely different when eschatology posits an absolute goal at the end of the redemptive process corresponding to an absolute beginning of the world in creation; for then, no longer a segment but the whole sweep of history is drawn into one great perspective and the mind is impelled to view every part in relation to the whole. To do this means to construct a primitive theological system. Thus eschatology becomes the mother of theology and that first of all of theology in the form of a philosophy of redemptive history. While it is true that theology in the technical sense should not be sought in the Bible, because the appearance of it presupposes the completion of the process of revelation, nevertheless rudimentary preformations of it can be clearly discovered in certain Biblical writings. These emerge precisely where the mind of the organs of revelation becomes more or less clearly conscious of the historical structure of revelation, especially where this consciousness attains to the broad sweep of the eschatological vision. So we can speak of a theology of Isaiah and a theology of Paul, because in both the idea of redemption as a God-guided process moving to an appointed goal and rounded off in itself exercises a degree of unifying and systematizing influence on all their religious knowledge. The fundamental scheme of which this eschatological theology in early times, even before the New Testament period, avails itself is that of the two ages, the present age and the age to come, a scheme which has passed over from Jewish thought into New Testament teaching. In this developed form it is not found in the Old Testament. But the substance is found there, and, what is even more important, this substance has in one passage of the Old Testament created for itself another form in the distinction between the two *beriths*, the old *berith* made at Sinai and the new *berith* to be made in the future. This distinction, where it occurs in Jeremiah, has eschatological significance; it is not the meaning of the prophet that the new *berith* which is promised may in course of time have to give way to a newer one; the consciousness lying back of this utterance differs essentially from the earlier consciousness, which counted a succession of *berith*s one replacing another. To the prophet the future *berith* promised is a final and absolute arrangement, beyond which in the perfection and permanence of its appointments nothing can be conceived. It gathers into itself all the wealth of eschatological expectation. The distinction between it and the old *berith* assumes for Jeremiah the character of a great bi-section of history; and at the beginning of each of the periods thus distinguished stands a fundamental redemptive self-disclosure of God. It is this idea of a succession of two *berith*s that has yielded the earliest and the inspired form of the philosophy of redemption—a form older than the doctrine of the two ages. But the peculiarity of Hebrews consists in this, that it brings into fructifying contact these two distinctions, that between the present age and the age to come and that between the first covenant and the second covenant. The new διαθήκη is to the writer of Hebrews as little as it was to Jeremiah something temporary and provisional. It embodies the consummation of all the work of God for His people; it is the ocean into which all the rivers of history roll their waters from the beginning of the world. Although the first covenant does not quite coincide with the first age, since it dates from Sinai and the first age began with creation, yet in regard to the second covenant and the age to come there is complete identification; those who are under the one are in principle in the other; Christians do taste the powers of the age to come and have arrived at the eschatological Mount Zion, the heavenly Jerusalem, the city of the living God. The revelation of the New Covenant is not only better comparatively speaking; it is final and eternal because delivered in a Son, than whom God could send no higher revealer. That the New Covenant actually has this comprehensive eschatological significance, and is not a mere soteriological episode, is easily obscured by the prominent place which the ideas of priesthood and sacrifice with their typical antecedents in the history of Israel occupy, whereby it might appear as if for the writer they formed merely a counterpart of what was characteristic of a definite historical development, and so themselves also were to be regarded in the same light. What corresponds to an intervening episode may seem to partake of the nature of an intervening episode. This would be a false inference if for no other reason than that the author counts the priesthood and sacrifice of Christ among the eternal realities. But the error may also be corrected by observing that in the opening chapters of the Epistle, where the outcome rather than the process of the Christian salvation is dwelt upon, a form of statement prevails which represents Christianity as the counterpart and fulfilment of the original order of things instituted at creation. The New Covenant as the goal of God's special dealings with man is determined by the point of departure of this divine procedure in the primeval state of man. The Christian order of things, the great salvation as the author calls it, involves according to the second chapter subjection of the entire οἰκουμένη to mankind. And this subjection is described in words of the eighth Psalm, a creation-Psalm which relates to the world-rule God at the beginning placed before man as his destiny. The implication therefore is, that in the new οἰκουμένη this original destiny of mankind is first realized through. Christ The 14th verse of the same chapter speaks of redemption as deliverance from the power and fear of death and from the devil who reigns through death, a representation which clearly points back to the account of the temptation and fall of man. Again in the fourth chapter, where the Christian state of salvation appears as a "rest", the author, though in part speaking of this in terms derived from the rest of Canaan, nevertheless finds its deeper and ultimate basis in the rest of God, the σαββατισμός, which crowned the creation of the world.

The New Covenant then coincides with the age to come; it brings the good things to come; it is incorporated into the eschatological scheme of thought. Such a way of looking at the Christian state is, of course, not confined to the Epistle to the Hebrews. Other writers of the New Testament, especially Paul, are quite familiar with this point of view and not infrequently represent even the present life of the believer on earth as semi-eschatological, as an anticipation in principle of the conditions of the life to come. But the difference between this and what we meet with in Hebrews should not be overlooked. Paul does not apply this train of thought to the idea of the covenant, the Epistle to the Hebrews does. As a result, what Paul gives in his distinction between the present world and the world to come and in the equation of Christianity with the latter is a religious philosophy of the history of the race in general. The present age and the present world stand for the reign of sin and evil, "the flesh", as Paul calls it; the age or world to come is the realm of redemption, the reign of the Spirit. "The present age" and "the present world" always have for Paul an evil connotation: the two eras of eschatology are ethically contrasted. The writer of Hebrews on the other hand, by specifically equating the world to come with the New Covenant, is led to identify the first age with the first covenant. The distinction between the two ages is drawn entirely within the sphere of redemption and revelation and the primitive philosophy or theology attaching itself to this distinction becomes specifically a philosophy of redemption and revelation. While the conception produced by this inter-marriage between the covenant-idea and eschatology is not so great and sweeping as the Pauline scheme, it represents within its narrower limits a most valuable positive supplement to the more negative outlines of redemptive history as drawn by Paul.

The service rendered by the author of Hebrews in this field is not, however, confined to the recognition of the principles of progress, comprehensiveness and finality inherent in the covenant-idea. Profound perceptions as these are, they do not touch the fundamental problem of the philosophy of history, which is likewise the basic problem of the philosophy of redemption and revelation. It is not enough to know that history moves towards a goal; the great question, without the solution of which the thinking mind cannot rest satisfied, concerns the element of identity in the flux of development. What is the stable, the constant substance that underlies the ceaseless never-resting change? To what extent and where and in what form is the goal that beckons at the end present at the beginning? Derive the past and present all their value from the future, or do they contain a solid reality of eternal worth in themselves? These questions are urgently pressing in the sphere of religion, where the dignity of God and the dignity of man's spiritual relation to Him do not at any point allow the human subject and its Godward experience to be regarded as a mere transitory phase, a passing ripple on the surface of the stream. And they become most pressing of all when we enter the field of revealed religion, of special redemptive history, of the covenant of grace, where the bond between God and man becomes so intimate and precious that the postulate of a fixed essence inalterably the same through the ages will not be denied. God is not a God of the dead, but a God of the living; to Him all in all times must live; and an evolution which would leave no room for the presence in every one of its stages and moments of such a true life unto God is incompatible with the idea of religion itself. There is a catholicity of religion not merely in the form of space but as well in the form of time. It is the distinctive merit of the Epistle to the Hebrews that, in connection with its doctrine of the covenants, it has raised this great problem and found for it an answer that satisfies not only the religious mind in general but satisfies the heightened covenant-consciousness of the Christian believer in particular.

Let us briefly consider this solution and endeavor to trace the way in which the Epistle has arrived at it. The idea that the Old Covenant prefigures or foreshadows the content of the New does not of itself furnish it For the figure and the shadow are not the reality, and it is precisely for the reality during the time that they flitted across the scene of history that we are looking. Here again it is by the identification of the two covenants with the two ages and the two worlds of eschatology that the Epistle approaches the solution of the problem. In order to understand this we must recall the peculiar manner in which the older eschatology was affected by the Christian belief in the advent of the Messiah. Previous to Christianity the two ages and the two corresponding worlds were conceived as purely successive. The present age must come to an end before the coming age can have its beginning; the present evil world must pass away, before the coming perfect world can take its place; between the two no overlapping is conceivable. But no sooner has this scheme passed over on to Christian ground than a remarkable change in this very respect appears. The distinction between two chronologically successive stages becomes, in part at least, the distinction between two contemporaneous states or worlds. This is brought about by the appearance of the Christ and the accomplishment of His work. In Christian eschatology the Christ occupies from beginning to end the center of the stage. All developments, all transactions, all gifts, all experiences that make up the drama of the great world-change are related to Him and derive their significance from Him; He is the representative and exponent of the future life in its totality. "To be forever with the Lord" is the succinct expression of what the eschatological hope means to a Christian. But, where eschatology and the Christ are thus closely identified, there inevitably the appearance of the Christ and even the partial accomplishment of His work must be interpreted as ushering in the initial stage of the future world, the opening chapter of the life of eternity. We can actually observe this in Paul, who teaches that through the cross of Christ the

believer has been in principle snatched out of this present
evil world and translated into the eternal kingdom of the
Son of God's love. The resurrection of Christ is to the
Apostle the first act in the general resurrection that will
introduce the final kingdom of God. Christians have in effect
passed over from the age that is into the age to come. Their
commonwealth is above, where they sit with Christ in
heavenly places, and all that is necessary in the future is that
they shall undergo the last change which will make them, in
body as well as in soul, redeemed, supernatural,
eschatological creatures.

Now the point to which in this development our
attention should be directed concerns the resulting
coëxistence between two things that hitherto had been
considered purely successive. If the second world has
received its actual beginning through Christ, and if
nevertheless, as cannot be denied, the first world, this
present world, is still continuing in its course, then it is clear
that both now exist contemporaneously. From thinking of
the eschatological state as future the Christian mind is led to
conceive of it as actually present but situated in a higher
sphere. The horizontal, dramatic way of thinking gives place
in part to a process of thought moving in a perpendicular
direction and distinguishing not so much between before and
after, but rather between higher and lower. Within the
Epistles of Paul we can trace the gradual transition from the
one habit of thought to the other. Although the later

representation is in germ present from the beginning, and although the earlier is retained until the very last, yet, broadly speaking, the dramatic conception is more in evidence in the first group of Epistles, while the other view-point prevails in the Epistles of the first imprisonment. In the latter the contrast between here and there in a local sense, rather than between now and then in a chronological sense, prevails.

In the content of this higher world to which the Christian belongs two elements must be further distinguished. It is in part a product of the historical redemptive process. The completion of Christ's work and His return in glorified state to the heavenly sphere have first given this sphere its final character and as such it now exists alongside of this present lower world. But, of course, they have not created heaven. When the world to come was once identified with heaven the reflection lay near that it was not only existing now but had been existing previously to the Messianic epoch. The higher world was there from the beginning; it had a stable, original content, before it was affected by the appearance of the Messiah. Both these elements are recognized in the later Pauline teaching. The second one, that of the original existence of the main content of the heavenly life, finds expression in this, that Paul in the later Epistles speaks of the eschatological word not as having been produced or created but as having been revealed. The Christ Himself, who constitutes its center, shows in His life this twofold aspect in which it may be viewed. He belongs to it ever since it existed. His coming was an apokalypsis, a manifestation of its content. As a heavenly Being He abode upon the earth. But His resurrection and return to it likewise contributed to its perfecting. Thus it derives its being from the first and second creation alike. While, however, these two constituent elements of the higher world are clearly present with Paul, they are much more clearly and pointedly distinguished in the Epistle to the Hebrews. It is in Hebrews for the first time that conscious reflection is observed and positive emphasis placed upon the primordial, constant, stable existence of the higher world, antedating and overarching and outlasting all temporal developments, a world of the αἰώνιον, not subject to change and harboring the supreme realities. Hebrews recognizes, with Paul, that the finale of the great drama of redemption in the death and ascension of Christ has put its impress upon the things above. The heavenly sanctuary was cleansed; through Christ's sacrifice the spirits of just men were made perfect; He carried with His new life the supreme form of the rest of God into the Sabbath that had been celebrated above from the beginning. Still the main stress is laid on the other side, on the fact that in reality all along the world to come had preëxisted in its heavenly form. The chronological relation is reversed; that which in course of historical development appeared the last was in a deeper and truer sense the first. Broadly speaking the Christian things are not a new product

of time; they are rather the descent into time of the essence
of eternity. We touch here upon what expositors are
accustomed to call the Alexandrianism of the Epistle and in
which they recognize the influence of Philo and of the older
Platonic speculation with its distinction between the two
worlds, that of ideas and that of sense, but what in our view
can better be explained as the direct outcome of the internal
development of Christian eschatology itself.

We shall now be prepared to understand how the
recognition, that the two worlds exist and have existed side
by side from the beginning, enables the author of Hebrews
to solve the chief problem of the history of redemption and
revelation. For it is in Hebrews that the first age and the first
world are identified with the first covenant. When,
therefore, the question is raised, how the Old Covenant can
be identical in substance with the New, what is the common
essence, that notwithstanding the great progress from the
one to the other, makes them two coherent stages in the
expression and conveyance of the same spiritual reality, the
answer is immediately forthcoming: that same world of
heavenly spiritual realities, which has now come to light in
the Person and work of Christ, already existed during the
course of the Old Covenant, and in a provisional typical way
through revelation reflected itself in and through
redemption projected itself into the religious experience of
the ancient people of God, so that they in their own partial
manner and measure had access to and communion with and

enjoyment of the higher world, which has now been let down and thrown open to our full knowledge and possession. In other words, the bond that links the Old and the New Covenant together is not a purely evolutionary one, inasmuch as the one has grown out of the other; it is, if we may so call it, a transcendental bond: the New Covenant in its preëxistent, heavenly state reaches back and stretches its eternal wings over the Old, and the Old Testament people of God were one with us in religious dignity and privilege; they were, to speak in a Pauline figure, sons of the Jerusalem above, which is the mother of all.

This is a profounder solution than is offered in the well-known formula of Augustine: "the New Testament is latent in the Old, the Old Testament lies open in the New". More profound, because, together with the statement of the fact, it gives the reason for the fact. The latent existence of the verities and potencies of the Christian religion in the old dispensation are due to no other cause than that the Christian religion lived even at that time as redemptive truth and redemptive power in the heavenly world and from there created for itself an embryonic form of existence in the life of Israel. The writer of Hebrews would have subscribed to the belief that Christianity is as old as Abraham and as old as Moses, nay as old as Paradise, because it is heaven-born and not the child of earth.

In a variety of ways the Epistle gives expression to this truth. First of all in what it teaches about the Old Testament forms of religion as partaking of the nature of shadows, σκίαι. It is easy to miss the exact meaning of this, because it is often too rashly identified with the Pauline formula containing the same figure: "which are a shadow of the things to come but the body is Christ's" (Col. 1:17), and which yet is quite differently oriented. Paul in thus formulating it thinks along the horizontal line of historic development: the shadow is the obscure outline which the reality approaching through time casts before itself. Hence the correlative to the shadow is the body. The author of Hebrews on the other hand lets his thought move along the perpendicular line that runs from heaven to earth: the shadow is a shadow not of something that comes after, but of something that lies above; it is not cast before, but reflected down; hence its correlate is not the body, but the εἰκών, the image, by which is meant the celestial prototype. According to ch. 10:1 the law has the shadow of the good things of the world to come, not the image itself. That image the New Covenant possesses; but it existed in the presence of God in heaven when He gave the law to Israel, and from it the shadow came forth which the law presents. True, the Old Testament forms also prefigure what is to follow in the line of historic emergence, they are forecasts in the Pauline sense, but they are this only because first they are reflexes of a heavenly reality which was destined at the end of the ages to come down to earth and fill the New Covenant. If the painter first draws a sketch from the work of art that lives in his inner vision, and then projects the picture from its spiritual form of existence into the form of canvas and color, the sketch will be a prophecy of the finished painting, precisely because it was a shadow of the picture in concept. In a somewhat similar sense the author of Hebrews means by shadow the sketch which God drew on the ceremonial canvas of the law of the eternal things that form the object of His vision in the world above. In another passage (8:5) this is said in so many words. Here we read that the Old Testament priests serve that which is a copy and a shadow (ὑπόδειγμα καὶ σκιά) of the heavenly things. The term "copy" explains the term "shadow" and both are equally related to a celestial reality. But perhaps even more strikingly the author's way of thinking in this respect reveals itself in the peculiar use he makes of the ideas of type and antitype. He follows in this matter a terminology which is apt to be confusing to the ordinary reader, because it apparently is the opposite of that usually combined with these words. We say, as a rule, that the Old Covenant has the type, the New Covenant the antitype. And this is Scriptural; for the Apostle Peter so conceives of it when he represents the water of the deluge as the type, the water of baptism as the antitype (1 Pet. 3:21). And yet the author of Hebrews distinctly tells us (9:24) that the Old Testament tabernacle was the antitype, not the type. The explanation is very simple. It lies in this, that antitype means copy, that which is fashioned after the type, and the Old Testament tabernacle was copied, fashioned after the tabernacle in heaven. Likewise the author also finds it significant that Moses was shown a type, a model of the sanctuary on the Mount, (8:5 cpr. with Ex. 25:40.) And all the Old Testament things in general are in this sense called copies of the things in the heavens (9:23).

Still another means of tracing the author's view of the relation between the heavenly world and the make-up of the Old Testament religion is afforded in the peculiar meaning he attaches to the predicate ἀληθινός, translated in the English versions by "true", but more adequately rendered by "veritable". This is a predicate reserved for the things in heaven because, in contrast to the shadows of the Old Covenant, they constitute the solid reality, the veritable substance. In this characteristic use of the word ἀληθινός Hebrews coincides, with the Fourth Gospel. There the Evangelist speaks of the Logos as "the true light" and our Lord calls Himself "the true vine", "the true bread", and defines the latter as "the bread that comes down out of heaven, the bread of God" (6:33). And even more closely approaching the view-point of Hebrews is the contrast drawn in the prologue between the law given through Moses, and the grace and truth which came through Jesus Christ, for here, it will be observed, the Christian revelation is characterized as "truth" in distinction from the Mosaic law to which this predicate does not belong. The meaning is not, of course, that the Mosaic law is untrue or false in the ordinary sense of the word; in fact this misunderstanding is carefully guarded against by the form of statement employed: the law was given "through" Moses, which implies that Moses in the lawgiving was only the instrument of God, from whom nothing false or untrue can come. "Truth" here means what it means in Hebrews; it expresses the heavenly character of the Christian realities of revelation and redemption in which the higher world directly communicates itself, and the opposite of "the true" is the typical, wherein the connection with the heavenly world is present only in a mediated, shadowy form. And Jesus, because He is the center and exponent of this great projection of the supernatural into the lower world is called "the Truth". In the well-known answer to Thomas concerning the way to the place whither Jesus is going, our Saviour declares that He Himself personally is the way. His way is into heaven, and through identification with Him the disciples can reach the same goal. But our Lord further explains this fact, that the way to heaven lies through Him, from His being "the truth", and "the life", which means nothing else than that the veritable higher world has come down in Him, and that particularly the heavenly life has made its appearance on earth in His Person. All this is but the statement in a more general form of what the Epistle to the Hebrews affirms with specific reference to the sphere of priesthood and sacrifice.

A couple of very instructive examples of the twofold relation in which the Epistle places the things of the Old Covenant as on the one hand looking upward to the world of heaven, on the other hand looking forward to the New Covenant, may be found in what it teaches about the figure of Melchizedek and about the conception of the promised rest. In the historical sequence of things Christ is said to be a priest after the order of Melchizedek. Here we have the ordinary correspondence between type and antitype, the former pertaining to the Old the latter to the New Covenant. To Melchizedek belongs the first, to Christ the later appearance on the scene of history. But in the third verse of the eighth chapter the author reverses this relation, representing it in this way, that not Christ was made like unto Melchizedek, but, on the contrary, Melchizedek was made like unto the Son of God. The introduction of the name "Son of God" here is highly significant. It describes Christ in His divine, eternal nature. From this eternal life that places the Son of God above all time and history, the eternity-character enveloping Melchidezek in the record of Genesis was copied, that thus delineated he might again in the time-perspective of history prefigure the historic Christ. The same observation may be made with regard to the "rest" promised the people of God. The rest of the land of Canaan given to Israel of old was a type of the supreme rest opened up by Jesus in the New Covenant. But this rest of Canaan was by no means the first or original embodiment of the religious idea of rest. Back of it and above it lay in the heavenly world the "sabbatismos" of God spoken of in the account of creation, and which is identical with the Christian rest, since believers are received by God into the rest that is His own. Generalizing this we may say that according to the teaching of the Epistle the Old Testament things are both copies and copied from, and the latter because they are the former.

It needs, after what has been said, no lengthy demonstration to show that Hebrews vindicates by this philosophy of history in the most satisfactory manner the identity and continuity of the Old Covenant with the New. Still it is not a work of supererogation to call attention to this. The concrete purpose for which the Epistle was written gave occasion for placing great emphasis on the superiority of the New Covenant to the Old. And this undoubtedly is also the proximate purpose in the mind of the author when he formulates that antithesis: there the shadow, here the image itself. But the antithesis would be overdrawn and the author's mark overshot if we were to interpret this as meaning: the old has only the shadow of the new. As we now know, the author's real intent is this: the old has only the shadow of heaven, the new has the full reality of heaven. And therefore to do the author full justice the stress should not be laid exclusively on the statement that there is "only" a shadow, but equally on the fact that there "is" a shadow of the true things of religion under the Old Covenant. The word in the prophets cannot take the place of the word in the Son, but it is a word in which God spoke. The sacrifices and lustrations could not do the work for which alone the priestly work of Christ is adequate, but they were in their own sphere faithful adumbrations and true means of grace, through which a real contact with the living God was actually maintained. When again and again, in pursuance of the immediate end in view, the author declares their weakness and unprofitableness (7:18), this is meant comparatively, but is not intended to void them of all religious efficacy. If taken in an absolute sense, such statements would warrant the inference that the Old Covenant had no spiritual substance at all, that the saints of old moved wholly among shadows, for which no body was yet in existence. This would be the same erroneous impression that is sometimes derived in an even stronger degree from the Pauline statements in which the Apostle speaks of the religious life under the law, statements which seem to allow nothing for this life in the way of positive spiritual privilege and enjoyment, and dwell only on the condemnatory, cursing, slaying function of the law. And yet we know from Paul that he was well-acquainted not only with the objective foreshadowing which the facts of the Christian redemption had found in the Old Covenant but also with the subjective prelibations which had been tasted by the saints of those days. And so it is in Hebrews. With whatever degree of clearness or dimness they might themselves apprehend the fact, God stood in spiritual relations to the people of Israel, they were not cut off from the fount of life and blessedness. Through the shadows and ceremonies and all the instrumentalities of the flesh, God controlled with a sure and sovereign hand the religious destinies of each member of His covenant people. Not only under the influence of special inspiration were a David and other Psalmists or a Jeremiah enabled to take to themselves prophetic draughts of the waters of life, which their vision saw springing up in the coming age, there was a direct and contemporaneous interaction between the redemptive approaches of God in the religious forms of that day and the believing and unbelieving responses with which they were met on the part of man. Instructive in this respect is the description given by the author of the dealings of God with the people during the wilderness journey and the people's attitude during that journey to the rest that had been promised. So far as the form was concerned, this promise had come to them only through the medium of the σάρξ; it was enveloped in the prospect of the inheritance of the land of Canaan that God had held out from of old and renewed at the time of their redemption from Egypt. And yet it is clearly the author's conviction that far deeper and more tremendous issues were decided on that occasion with reference to each of the participants in the history than the mere question, who of them would survive to enter the promised land. Through the shadowy forms, in the midst of which the actors moved, a great drama of belief and unbelief was enacted, the outcome of which was by God reckoned decisive in the eternal sphere. It was not only from the typical but from the everlasting rest that the unbelievers were excluded, when God swore that fearful oath that they should not enter in. And those who believed were then and there given the right of entrance into all that the divine rest did mean and would come to mean in the future. The author is so vividly impressed with this that he does not content himself with comparing this Old Testament method of procedure with the method now pursued under the new dispensation but approaches the comparison from the opposite end. He does not say: *they* as well as *we*, but *we* as well as *they* have had an evangel preached unto us, whence also he is able to hold up the unbelief of the Israelites as a warning example to the readers of his own day. No more striking proof than this could be afforded of the fact, that he regarded the same spiritual world with the same powers and blessings as having evoked the religious experience of the Old and the New Testament alike.

Having thus traced the influence of the idea of the covenant on the Epistle's view of revelation, we next enquire whether the same influence can be discovered within the other hemisphere of teaching, that relating to the priesthood and sacrifice of Christ. The author consciously coordinates this with the doctrine of Jesus' revealing function: these two taken together constitute for him the full orb of the official significance of our Lord. He calls Christ "the apostle and high-priest of our confession" (4:1).

The two terms are subsumed under one article so as to bring out their intimate coherence. Moreover in this their conjunction they are made the substance of the Christian confession, which presupposes alike their fundamental and comprehensive character. Finally, the readers are invited to consider Him in this twofold capacity, and this means that not merely in objective doctrinal presentation but in the practical experience of what Jesus is and does for them these two categories stand out prominently before their minds.

This precludes our regarding the idea of the priesthood of Christ in the light of a novelty first conceived by the author of the Epistle. It must have been familiar to the readers; and this appears from the fact that they are charged with a lack of proficiency in Christian understanding because of their failure to perceive the significance of Melchizedek in his typical relation to the priesthood of Christ. And yet, what seems to have been familiar in the circle to which the Epistle addresses itself does not appear with the same sharp delineation anywhere else in the New Testament. No doubt the substance of the teaching embodied in it was common Christian property; only this substance seems nowhere to have taken the form that Christ is and acts as a priest. Leaving out of account the well-known passage in the Apocalypse, in which certain parts of the high-priestly apparel are introduced into the description of the glorified Christ, there is no New Testament statement outside of Hebrews which explicitly calls Jesus a priest. Since, therefore, much that is subsumed under the priesthood of Christ in Hebrews is likewise present in the other writings, and yet has not there resulted in investing Him with the office of a priest, it clearly follows that there must have existed in the minds of our author a specific reason for expressing in terms of priesthood what could be expressed and was commonly expressed without the use of this title. Besides the common conception of the Saviour's sacrificial, expiatory work there must have been a peculiar point of view, an original turn given to the old established belief, a certain plus in the apprehension of Jesus' saving significance, and to this it must be due, that the idea of priesthood comes to the front. This peculiar element we must endeavor to discover, and in it, if we mistake not, will be seen the mutual adjustment between the covenantal aspect of religion and the Saviour's priestly office.

It will be best to proceed analytically, i.e., by resolving the conception of priesthood into its constituent elements. The Epistle makes this easy for us by the degree of reflexion almost approaching to definition which in one passage it expends upon the idea (5:1 ff). The first element entering into the office is that of "representation of man with God": "Every high priest … is appointed for men in things pertaining to God". The movement of the priestly function is in a direction opposite to that of the prophetic function. The prophet officiates from God to man, the priest officiates from man to God, represents man with God. This at least is, broadly speaking, the case, although there are some aspects of the priestly task in which, after the culmination of its God-ward movement, it turns back, as it were, upon itself and conveys from God to man such things as the priestly benediction, forgiveness and help. In the main, however, the Epistle remains true to its own definition: the priest takes care for man of the things pertaining to God.

Closely connected with this is the second requisite of the office which we may define as "solidarity" with those represented. Here again the priesthood differs from the prophetic office. We have already seen how strongly the Epistle, in describing Christ's revealing function, emphasizes His eternal sonship, His divine nature. It is different where His priestly work is concerned. Here He represents man, and His qualification is measured by His nearness to man. The author, therefore, does not fail to include this in the definition: Every high priest, "being taken from among men", is appointed for men. The work is of such a kind that it cannot be performed by any one who stands outside of the circle he is called upon to represent. Angels can serve as revealing organs, ministering servants, but they are not qualified for acting in the priesthood. It is of importance to notice this point, because in Judaism the tendency to interpose angelic beings between God and man from fear that a direct contact with the creature would injure the divine majesty, showed its influence not merely upon the manward movement of revelation but likewise in the

Godward movement of the priesthood, as when the archangel Michael is represented as officiating at the altar in the heavenly sanctuary. Over against such a view Hebrews insists upon it, that there must exist antecedent solidarity between the priest and the people. And the author conceives of this solidarity on deeper lines than is commonly appreciated. It is customary to say that he insists upon the possession by Christ of our human nature as essential to His priestly representation of us. But this is not saying enough. The line of reasoning followed in the second chapter shows plainly that the solidarity lies back of this, that the assumption of human nature through the incarnation is not its basis but only a form in which the principle asserts itself. When we are told that "both he that sanctifies and they that are being sanctified are all of one" (2:11), it would be a mistake to interpret this phrase "of one" of the common descent of Christ with us from Adam or Abraham. That something else is meant the working out of the idea in the sequel convincingly shows. For the author proceeds to prove the fact of this solidarity from the observation that Christ calls believers His spiritual brethren, and that He resembles them by assuming the same trustful attitude towards God which marks them as children of God, nay that He Himself sustains to them the relation of a father to his children. All this lies in the spiritual sphere and while, in its concrete form, not possible without the incarnation, is not in principle caused by it. On the contrary the author represents the incarnation as the further carrying out of a spiritual solidarity already given: "Since then the children are sharers in flesh and blood, He also Himself in like manner partook of the same" (2:14). The joint-sonship of Christ with believers does not follow from the incarnation, it produces the incarnation: because those with whom He was spiritually identified, those whom He resembled in sonship, partook of flesh and blood, He carried His solidarity with them to the point of the assumption of their nature. It is obvious that the root of the identification of Christ with us which underlies His priesthood is sought in His standing before God, in the divine appointment by which His destiny and the destiny of the people of God were forever united. It is what the old theology used to call the federal oneness of Christ with believers that is here taught. That this idea is actually in the writer's mind follows from one striking feature in the representation which is often overlooked. Believers are not merely called joint-children of God with Christ, but are called "children of Christ". The writer puts upon the lips of Jesus the Isaianic utterance: "Behold I and the children whom God has given me" (2:13) and joins to this the affirmation that, because the children, i.e. Christ's children, were partakers of flesh and blood, He also Himself in like manner partook of the same. They were His children because back of all temporal developments in either His birth or their birth, they had been given to Him of the Father. He stands not only in general solidarity with them, but in that specific form of solidarity which constitutes Him the Father and them the children—a representation which, is unique in the New Testament, where believers are elsewhere called the children of God and not the children of Christ.

While thus resting on a federal basis and carrying with itself the incarnation, the solidarity extends to the further concrete aspects of the human life of Christ. "It behooved Him in all things to be made like unto His brethren" (2:17). In these words the author for the first time touches upon the subject which later is repeatedly reverted to: the identification of Christ with us in the common experiences of human life, especially in those common experiences that belong to the sphere of weakness, suffering and temptation. It is a favorite motif of the modern theology, to find in this a sign of reaction from the increasing deification of Christ in the early church with its tendency to dehumanize Him and to bury the historic Jesus under the rank growth of mythology and speculation. Hebrews is then given the credit, together with the Synoptic Gospels, of having rescued for us the human Christ from the danger of entire obliteration. This rests on a misapprehension of the facts. So far as the intent of Hebrews is concerned, the feature in question certainly has nothing to do with the desire to do justice to the humanity of Christ for its own sake. The motive is a strictly doctrinal one; it is for the sake of the Saviour's priesthood, as a functional necessity, that His solidarity with believers in nature and experience is emphasized: "It behooved Him in all things to be made like unto His brethren" to the end "that He might be a merciful and faithful high priest in things pertaining to God, to make propitiation for the sins of the people" (2:17).

The third element entering into the priestly function is that of "offering". This also the author includes in the definition: "Every high priest being taken from among men is appointed for man in things pertaining to God, that He may offer both gifts and sacrifices for sins." In connection with the term "sacrifice" we are inclined to think too narrowly of the slaying of the victim. To do so leaves out of account an act of co-equal if not of greater importance in the ritual. For this reason it is better to avail ourselves, as the author throughout does, of the verb "to offer" which, owing to the peculiar point of view from which it regards the transaction, is precisely adapted to call to mind that which follows the death of the sacrifice. Where the author refers to the offering of Christ, he by no means restricts the range of this act to what happened on Calvary; to his view the offering was not finished there; its culminating stage lay in the self-presentation of Christ or in the presentation of His blood, as it is variously expressed, before God in heaven. Sometimes he even refers to this latter act, not as a part or the climax of the offering, but as "the offering" par excellence. And what is true of the offering is true of the "expiation". This also is not confined to the cross: Christ expiates in heaven as well as on Calvary. Evidently the process as a whole is covered by the terms, which consequently can be applied to each half of it, yet so that the second stage more clearly brings out its real significance and throws back its light upon the first. The death of Jesus, no less than His appearance in heaven, the Epistle places under the aspect of an offering, a movement of self-presentation to God: there is a continuous approach realizing itself in two steps. At this point the ritual conception of Hebrews differs from that of the Old Testament law. In the law the slaying of the animal is not the act of the priest, but of the man who brings the sacrifice for himself. The two acts of the offering, that of the slaying of the victim, and that of the presentation of the blood, here fall to two different persons, the former to the bringer of the sacrifice, the latter to the priest. In Hebrews, on the other hand, the priest performs both. Nor is this an insignificant variation from the Old Testament rule made necessary by the fact that no distinct person, apart from Christ, existed who could act in the capacity of the giver of the sacrifice. For the whole trend of the Epistle's teaching, which is towards laying the scene of Christ's priestly function in heaven, would naturally have predisposed the author for representing Him in connection with His death on earth, not as a priest, but merely as a sacrifice. When notwithstanding this, as we shall see, he insists upon it that Jesus officiated as priest at His own death, there must be a positive reason for this. Two motives probably coöperated towards leading his mind in this direction. In the first place, the close identification of Christ with the people on whose behalf the offering is brought made it appear natural that He should act as their representative at this point also. He is not merely priest and victim in one, but also plays the part of the Old Testament giver; through Him the people of God bring to the altar the required gift that is to make covering for their sin. He represents us both in dying and in offering Himself to die. And, in the second place, the ministry of Christ as priest at His own death helps to bring out a principle considered by the author of the Epistle as of the highest importance, this principle viz., that the surrender of Christ to death was a spiritual, voluntary one. While ascribing real efficacy to the death of Jesus, the Epistle does not attribute this to the death as a mere passive, physical experience. The blood, the death were necessary, but as bare physical things they were not enough; they derive their ultimate value from the concomitant psychical state. What renders the death effectual is precisely that which distinguishes it from the death of the Old Testament sacrifices, which was a purely passive and physical experience. It was impossible that the blood of bulls and goats should take away sins (10:4) and therefore a different sacrifice had to be provided; for the death suffered without a will, there is substituted the death of Christ, which was the doing of the will of God by the will of the sacrifice: "Sacrifice and offering thou wouldst not; a body didst thou prepare for me; … then said I, lo, I am come to do thy will, O God". "By that will we have been sanctified through the self-presentation (προσφορά verse

10) of the body of Jesus Christ once for all." In 9:13, 14 also
the blood of goats and bulls and the blood of Christ are put
in contrast from the same point of view. The one operates in
the sphere of the flesh, because it is an offering of flesh, the
other cleanses the conscience, because it is an offering of
Spirit. Hence also there is a further difference in the
necessity of their respective operations: the argument is à
fortiori: "how much more shall the blood of Christ cleanse
your consciences". The animal offerings under the old
covenant cleansed even the flesh not so much through any
inherent necessity, but in result of a sovereign appointment
of God. It is different with the sacrifice of Christ: His blood
operates in the sphere of the conscience, not merely because
God sovereignly appoints for it such an effect, or
condescends to attribute to it such value, but because in the
eternal nature and constitution of things such effect and
value are inseparably connected with it. The offering of
Christ is an αἰώνιον because it brought to God eternal
Spirit, a sacrifice of self, brought by a divine Person, who as
such alone has the absolute right to dispose of Himself,
because He is absolutely His own. Now it seems that in
order to give emphasis to this important train of thought the
author joins to the passion of Christ as an offering the action
of Christ as a priest. It is as priest that He represents the
spiritual, voluntary, spontaneous side of the transaction. It is
as priest that He carries into the sacrifice that inward God-
seeking and God-reaching movement which from the

beginning makes it a true gift to the Father. It is a striking confirmation of this that in the passage last quoted the author does not say: Christ offered Himself "as" eternal Spirit, as in the context it might have been expected, but "through" eternal Spirit He offered Himself. It is not only what was offered, but through what it was offered that determined the efficacy. And precisely this category of "thoroughness" is represented by the priesthood.

The offering of Jesus is specifically connected with the fact of sin, as the author's definition again takes pains to remind us: "Every high priest being taken from among men is appointed for men in things pertaining to God, that he may offer both gifts and sacrifices for sins". In this statement, it is true, the offering of "gifts" and the offering of "sacrifices for sins" are distinguished, and from this it has been inferred, that there is a side to the priestly function that has no connection with sin. This inference is unwarranted. The only thing that the distributive form of the statement implies is that not all priestly offerings are sin-offerings, that is, offerings for the direct and main purpose of expiation. Besides these there are "gifts" intended for consecration. But that does not prove the coming of these gifts of consecration through a priest, to be the normal thing, so that even in a sinless state a priesthood would be required to offer the gifts of consecration to God. That a man cannot in his own person bring even his gift of consecration to the altar is due to no other cause than his sinfulness. The defilement of sin not merely requires expiation; it also precludes personal approach of whatever kind to God. The definition, therefore, means nothing else than that the priest exists for offering gifts to God on account of the fact of sin, and sacrifices to God for the expiation of sin. It is, of course, in the abstract quite possible to conceive of a representative head of unfallen humanity furnishing the point of contact between the race and God, gathering up in Himself the united concerns of men with God, voicing their religious approach to God in its various forms of expression. Serious doubt, however, may be felt as to whether the ideal relation of man to God in a sinless state ought not to be so direct and immediate as to forbid the interposition of a priest between him and God. The representative position of Adam furnishes no true analogy, for here no religious approach to God on behalf of others is involved, as would be in the case of the priesthood. The difficulty might perhaps be met by conceiving of the Son of God as the hypothetical incumbent of this unsoteric priesthood in the state of rectitude; for the Son of God, as partaking of the divine nature, would not by His priesthood interfere with the immediacy of contact with God. We ought to realize, however, that, on the premises of the Epistle, such a construction would carry with itself the belief in the incarnation of Christ as contemplated in the normal order of the universe irrespective of the entrance of sin; for the Epistle, as we have seen, insists upon it, that a priest on behalf of mankind must partake of the nature of mankind. Consequently in the form which this theory of a hypothetical priesthood under a sinless régime has assumed, that advocated by Westcott, the incarnation of the Son of God is actually represented as in its ultimate analysis not contingent upon sin. Sin and redemption are a mere intervening episode in a scheme of things which made provision for a priesthood of the Son of God under all circumstances.

We need not pursue this line of speculation any further. It suffices to observe, that, if it lay at all in the mind of the writer, which cannot be disproven, it has left no trace upon the actual teaching of the Epistle. The priesthood of Christ is everywhere explained soteriologically. The very emphasis placed upon the sinlessness of Jesus as an indispensable qualification for the office indicates that His priesthood serves to accomplish something for sinners which sinners cannot accomplish for themselves. The difference between the Epistle and Philo lies precisely in this that the latter invests his Logos with a priestly function that is absolutely devoid of the expiatory element, whereas in Hebrews everything is staked on the thought of expiation. Close upon the definition of the priest in 5:1 follows the statement that he has to deal with the ignorant and erring, so that in the case of the Old Testament typical incumbent of the office his own sinfulness even became a helpful feature because, being compassed himself with infirmity and having to offer for his own sins no less than for the sin of the people, he was able to have a medium pathos (μετριοπαθεῖν), as the Epistle strikingly expresses it, that is to bear gently, to have patience with the failings of those whom he represented. In 2:17 "the things pertaining to God" are likewise more clearly defined by the following clause "to make propitiation for the sins of the people". And even where the unending duration of the Saviour's priesthood, as typified by Melchizedek, is dwelt upon, and where consequently the eternal perspective might most easily have suggested to the author the final surmounting of every thought of sin and redemption, this result does not follow, but the writer continues to speak in soteriological terms no less than in the other contexts relating more specifically to Christ's priestly work for the present. The effect of the eternal, unchangeable Melchizedek-priesthood is said to consist in this that He can save to the uttermost (i.e. either to the utmost point of time or to the utmost degree) by making everlasting intercession. By entering into the heavenly holy place, which is the central act of His priestly work, He obtained eternal redemption. The redemption also is an αἰώνιον. Over the entire eternal world, so far as the author's vision extends, redemption spreads its wings not as a dark shadow, but as a glorious consciousness capable of being perpetuated, because from it the pain of sin is forever removed by the superabundant expiation. The saints above breathe forever the atmosphere of grace.

As a matter of fact, where the Epistle means to contemplate the Saviour's eternal significance, under a not-specifically redemptive aspect, but from the point of view of a carrying into effect of the original destiny of creation, the author avails himself for this purpose of another conception than that of the priesthood. In such connections he represents the Son as the "Heir" of all things. As the world was made through Him, so the world was made for His inheritance. This corresponds strictly to Paul's teaching that Christ is the goal of creation. To Him the inhabited earth that is to come (οἰκουμένη μέλλουσα, 2:5) has been made subject. To be sure, in the historical outcome of the world-process, this also has been fulfilled in a form which is not independent of sin and redemption, because it has been realized through the incarnate Christ, and as a crowning reward for the suffering of death. But from the concrete, actual form of fulfilment we can here distinguish the general possibility of the inheritance of the world as such which, had no sin entered, would not have required the incarnation of the Son of God and might have been a glorious eternal reality. To be priest over the race the Son would have to be incarnate; the sovereignty over the eschatological world He could have received, if the element of sin be discounted, without the assumption of our human nature.

The next element to be taken into account in the analysis of the conception of priesthood is that of "leadership and participation in attainment". The priest is not one who stands personally outside of the movement he directs or has no share of his own to realize in the end he serves. His close unity with the people and his representative relation to them already indicate that the opposite must be true. The Epistle emphasizes that the priest himself is the first to travel the road and reach the goal to which it is his task to bring others. In the definition of the priest that has so far guided us this element also is referred to: a priest is one who "is bound, as for the people, so also for himself, to offer for sins". It is true, in applying the definition to Christ, this particular feature cannot be transferred from the Old Testament high priest to Him without restriction. For the Aaronic high priest is sinful and therefore in the most literal sense and along the whole line of his own ministry partakes of the expiating and saving effect of the same. Jesus is the sinless One, nay, to the efficacy of His priestly work His separateness from sin is absolutely essential. None the less the Epistle upholds the general validity of the principle also with reference to Christ. Even in the case of the Old Testament high priest it was not his sinfulness which occasioned such a participation in the benefits of his office: the circumstance of his sinfulness only causes a trait that is inherent in the conception of the priesthood as such to stand out in clearer relief. The ideal priest, although not personally involved in sin, and consequently not capable of experiencing the cleansing of sin, must, with this one exception, share in the result he is set to accomplish. The Epistle does not hesitate to ascribe to Jesus, and that in His capacity as priest, the experience of salvation: He, a priest forever after the order of Melchizedek, having offered up in the days of His flesh prayers and supplications with strong crying and tears, unto Him that was able to save Him out of death, was heard for His godly fear, and so became the author of salvation unto all that obey Him (5:6–9). The Epistle employs two technical terms to express this precession of Christ on the pathway along which believers follow Him. The first term is ἀρχηγός occurring in two passages, 2:10 and 12:2. In the former Jesus is called "the ἀρχηγός of salvation"; in the latter "the ἀρχηγός of faith". The word can denote both the producer of an effect and the leader of a line; hence the twofold rendering of "author" and "captain". The context in each passage shows that both elements are represented in the pregnant meaning the author puts into the word, and that not by a purely external combination, but as resulting the one from the other. Jesus does not as an outside person procure salvation for the race; by breaking His own way to the goal He has carried the others in His wake. And again Jesus has not produced faith in us while Himself living above the plane and beyond the need of faith; it is through His own perfect exercise of faith that He helps believers to follow in His footsteps. This pregnant meaning of the word is also proved by the uses Peter makes of it in two passages recorded in Acts (3:15, 5:31) where he calls Jesus "the ἀρχηγός of life" and "an ἀρχηγός and σωτήρ". The rendering of the English versions "Prince of Life" and "Prince and Saviour", correctly brings out the thought that Jesus to the view of the Apostle through His resurrection was the first inheritor of life and at the same time the source of life to His followers. To the translators of the Authorized Version at least "prince" admirably rendered this, though it scarcely any longer conveys the idea to us, because, when that version was made, the etymology of prince from princeps, qui principium capit, was still perspicuous. He as a beginner took this life to Himself, and then opened it to others. In "Prince and Saviour" the two elements are distributed. Jesus is first of all the leader in salvation, then the giver of salvation. For the reason stated, in Hebrews the rendering "captain of salvation" and "captain of faith" is to be preferred to "author of salvation," "author of faith," because the function of a captain always suggests a degree of authorship, while the function of an author conveys no suggestion of leadership in the fruition of what is produced. The second term in which the same idea finds expression is even more illuminating for our present purpose because more directly connected with the Saviour's priestly work. In 6:20 the author calls Jesus πρόδρομος "forerunner" because as the first He has entered into that which is within the veil, and through that act of first entrance with His own blood has made it possible for us now to project our hope as an anchor of the soul into the same holy place and hereafter to follow Him in person.

The four ingredients of the conception of priesthood so far distinguished are by it naturally and easily held together.

We cannot, however, assert that for the expression of any single one of them, or even of all in their combination, the priestly formula is absolutely necessary. As a matter of fact we find all these ingredients, sometimes singly, sometimes variously combined, in other types of teaching, notably in Paul, where yet the formal concept of the priesthood of Christ does not emerge with them. That Christ's work has a God-ward reference, that He sustains a representative relation to believers, that in His lot both in the state of humiliation and in the state of glory He is closely identified with His people, that through the voluntary sacrifice of Himself in death He has wrought expiation, that as the first heir and participant of the eschatological state He leads us in the attainment unto glory—all these are characteristic Pauline ideas, and yet, as we have seen, the idea of the Saviour's priesthood does not become explicit in Paul. The point we must now notice is that in Hebrews all these ideas, while substantially identical with the corresponding trains of thought elsewhere, yet possess a physiognomy of their own. The cause of this is that in the mind of the author of Hebrews they are from the outset construed with reference to a very specific idea, the idea of approach unto God. It is towards this idea that the whole conception of the priesthood gravitates. A priest is one who brings his people into the divine presence. From this the feature that he is appointed in things pertaining to God receives its more concrete interpretation. The God-ward reference of his office is not an abstract logical one, but that of a real movement of life. That he represents man and is identified with man to the extent of assuming human nature looks towards the same end. It is true, this was also necessary for and is explained by the Epistle from the vicarious death of Jesus: He partook of flesh and blood that through death He might bring to naught him that had the power of death, and God prepared Him a body that He might fulfill the divine will through suffering (2:14; 10:5). Still, the human nature of Jesus obtains its highest and final use in this that through it we are brought representatively into the presence of God: Christ entered into heaven to appear before the face of God for us (9:24). That He offers gifts and sacrifices for sins is in the last analysis directed towards the end that by the expiation all obstacles may be removed which prevent the sinner's access unto God. Finally that Jesus Himself shares in the outcome of His priestly ministry is fully accounted for by the fact that the sole purpose of this ministry is to come near unto God. Thus of the several elements into which the conception resolves itself all are seen to tend in the same direction and to propel each other with commulative force to the point where they reach their highest functional fulfilment in the priestly introduction of man into the immediate presence of God.

The correctness of the view taken may be verified by observing how it throws light on some outstanding features of the Epistle of which no very satisfactory explanation can otherwise be furnished. Two of these may here be briefly commented upon. The first has to do with the relative absence of a theory of atonement. In a writing which makes the priesthood and sacrifice of Jesus the center of its theme, one is à priori inclined to expect such a theory. On the whole the expectation is disappointed. Paul, with whom the sacrificial aspect of the death of Christ occupies a comparatively subordinate place, nevertheless offers far more in the line of a philosophy of sacrifice than the Epistle to the Hebrews. Various views have been taken of this surprising phenomenon. Some endeavor to deny its reality. They say: the author of Hebrews theorizes as much about the death of Christ as Paul does, only he does so in a different way and with different results. According to them the whole forensic frame of mind that underlies the Pauline soteriology is foreign to him. Paul looks upon sin as transgression, unrighteousness, entailing the curse of the law, and therefore as requiring penal suffering of a vicarious nature in order to expiation. The author of Hebrews looks upon sin as defilement, entailing exclusion from the presence of God and therefore as requiring lustration, cleansing. There is, as we shall see, a grain of truth in this form of statement, so far as the contrasted definition of the end of the atonement is concerned. But, when it offers itself as an exact reproduction of two contrasted theories as to the rationale of the process of atonement, it is utterly misleading. To impute to the author of Hebrews the view that sin is defilement which needs washing and that this is provided by the blood of Christ, is not to furnish him with a theory, that could be set over against the clean-cut doctrinal deliverances of Paul on the subject. The language of defilement and of lustration is figurative, symbolical language obviously borrowed from the Old Testament ceremonial law. But for this very reason it cannot take the place of a theory. When one wishes to explain on a theoretical basis how it is that the blood of Christ washes away sin, he has to reduce the physical figure to moral, spiritual factors; not the symbolism itself but only its spiritual counterpart is something that can be fairly placed by the side of the Pauline doctrine with a view to formulating a judgment on the agreement or disagreement of the two. To compare "washing" and "satisfaction", is as hopeless a procedure as to discuss the relative merits of baptism and regeneration as two distinct theories. Setting then this confusion of thought aside, we find that only two attempts have been made and can be made to make the symbolism truly commensurable with any other theory of atonement. The one lies in the direction of ritualism, the other in the direction of subjectivism. As to the former, it has been represented that the author was fully satisfied with the ritual transactions as such, that being impervious to their symbolic character he did not look for any deeper reason of their efficacy than the bare fact of their institution by God. That blood cleanses would, on this view, be a mystery of hieratic magic, and it would be quite legitimate to apeal to this as clear proof of the dependence of the teaching the Epistle on the contemporaneous mystery-religions. A moment's reflection shows how utterly untenable this standpoint is. The whole trend of Hebrews is away from ritualism and in the direction of spiritualizing. It is altogether incredible that a mind like the writer's should on this point, in flagrant inconsistency with its own genius as shown at every other point, have been satisfied with the blind of the shedding of blood without feeling the need of enquiry into its spiritual significance. It is true, the author reduces the necessity of the sacrifice of Christ to the will of God According to 10:5, 7, 10 the Messiah received a body He might be able to offer it up in death and thus fulfill will of God relative to His death. And in this will of God, carried out by Jesus, lies the cause of our sanctification. But it should be noticed that precisely in this context writer takes pains to emphasize the preferential and therefore reasonable character of the will of God in this respect. God set the execution of this His will by Christ above carrying out of His will embodied in the Old Testament law regarding animal sacrifice. Speaking in the word the Psalmist the Saviour says: "Sacrifice and offering Thou wouldest not, but a body didst Thou prepare for me; then said I, Lo, I am come to do thy will, O God ... taketh away the first, that he may establish the second." divine will, therefore, was not an arbitrary will, it had a reasonable content founded in the principles of the divinemind. Elsewhere also attention is called to the God-worthiness of the procedure of the atonement: there is in it a divine πρέπον, an intrinsic suitableness and decorum, it is in strict keeping with the nature and position of God as God: "For it behooved Him, for whom are all things through whom are all things, in bringing many sons to glory, to make the captain of their salvation perfect throught sufferings" (2:10). Still further, we have already seen that the contrast between the relative efficacy of the blood of the animal sacrifices of the Old Covenant as restricted to the sphere of the flesh and the absolute efficacy of the blood of Christ as applying to the sphere of the conscience is explicitly based on the intrinsic difference between the two transactions. The effect of Jesus' death was determined by His nature and attitude in regard to it: it was not then a blind act of ritual magic, but spiritualized through and through, which is but another way of saying that it stood in some intelligible relation to the divine necessities of the case, in other words, that objectively at least in the mind of God, and probably to the mind of the writer also, a philosophy of atonement lay back of the symbolism in which the teaching is clothed.

The other proposal lies in the direction of subjectivism. The attempt is made to differentiate between Paul's teaching on the death of Christ and that of Hebrews in this way, that the former puts the effect in the objective sphere of satisfaction of the divine justice, whereas the latter finds the effect within the heart and mind of man. The symbolism of defilement and cleansing would then find its spiritual counterpart in the moral change produced in man's subjective state. Some of the forms of statement employed by the Epistle with reference to the blood of Christ might, when interpreted according to the modern sound of the words, seem to favor this, as when the blood is said to purify and to sanctify and to render perfect. But no sooner do we bring to bear upon these modes of expression the light of strict, contextual exegesis than it is seen that they will not possibly bear such a subjectivizing interpretation. It is not the heart in the modern sense, nor the mind and will but the conscience, that is, the consciousness of sin, which is throughout regarded as the object of the purifying and sanctifying and perfecting influence of the death of Christ. The subjectivistic appearance of these phrases is delusive; in reality they pertain just as much to the objective sphere as the most characteristic Pauline phraseology. A difference in theory with Paul cannot be made out along this line.

What then is the true explanation of the self-restraint of the writer in respect to theorizing about the atonement? We believe it is simply as follows: The author deems it unnecessary to accentuate his theory of the atonement, partly because he takes for granted the vicarious theory of Paul, and all the time, while using the language of the ritual, in the background of his mind silently translates this into the terms of Pauline doctrine; but mainly because for the present moment he is far more interested in the outcome, the terminal point of the atoning process, than in its intrinsic operation. Looking at the atonement as a priestly ministry, the Epistle singles out for emphasis that aspect of it, in regard to which the priest is most in evidence. Not what the atonement is, but how Christ the priest makes it serve the supreme object of His office, this is the focus to which all the rays of light in the author's presentation of the subject are directed. And this explains not merely the negative feature of the relative absence of a theory; it also explains the peculiar terms in which the effect of the death of Christ is positively spoken of. For the terms above named "to purify", "to sanctify", "to render perfect", have this peculiarity that they all describe the death of Christ as instrumental in fitting the believer for that very thing to which it is the function of the priest to lead him. He is purified, that as being pure He may enter into the presence of God. He is sanctified, that in being holy he may live out his dedication to God. He is made perfect, that as being thoroughly equipped he may meet all the demands which the service of God imposes on him. In a word, the conception of the atonement is here subordinated to that of the purpose of the priesthood and viewed almost exclusively in relation to it.

This cannot be taken to prove, however, that the author in every connection lacked all interest in the working out of a theory of the reasonableness of the death of Christ. Every indication goes to show that he knew and cordially accepted the teaching of Paul in respect to this. In 9:12 we read of eternal redemption as having been obtained by the Saviour's offering; and redemption is an idea belonging to the vicarious train of thought. This redemption is further defined as a redemption away from the transgressions committed under the first covenant, the implication being that these transgressions, personified, held the Old Testament saints in bondage until they were ransomed from that bondage by the death of the Saviour. And in the twenty-eighth verse of the same chapter we meet with the most explicit substitutionary language: Christ was offered up to bear, that is, to take upon Himself, the sins of many, and shall appear a second time, apart from sin. This is language borrowed from Isa. 53:12 and it is almost identical with the statement borrowed by Peter from the same source (1 Pet. 2:24) "who His own self carried our sins in His body upon the tree", with this difference only, that by the local turn here given to the phrase in connection with the cross, the vicarious assumption of the sin of believers by Christ is more realistically brought out. The idea of substitution also clearly shines through in what is said about the purpose of our Lord's incarnation in 2:14. He partook of flesh and blood that He might be able to die, for it was through death only that death could be overcome. All these incidental modes of statement show that the author was quite familiar and in thorough sympathy with this central doctrine of the Pauline teaching. He makes no more of it simply because it lies to one side of the center of gravity in his conception of the priesthood.

The second interesting phenomenon in regard to which a similar observation may be made concerns the locality to which the Epistle assigns the priesthood of Christ. It is throughout represented as a priesthood exercised in heaven. The days of our Lord's flesh were the days of His perfecting, that is of His equipment for the office, and this equipment included the event of His death, so that the actual entrance upon the function lies beyond His earthly life and coincides with His entrance into heaven (2:17). He becomes a high priest for ever after the order of Melchizedek when He enters within the veil as our forerunner (6:20). In accordance with this He is called a minister of the sanctuary and of the true tabernacle which the Lord pitched, not man, so that, it would seem, His priesthood could have begun only when He entered that heavenly sanctuary (8:2). Even stronger is the statement made in the immediate sequel (8:4): "If He were on earth He would not be a priest at all, seeing there are those who offer the gifts according to the law". The question arises: how is all this to be reconciled with the other statements of the Epistle according to which Jesus made purification of sins before He ascended to the right hand of God (1:3), that in suffering without the gate He sanctified the people through His own blood (13:12), that He was manifested at the end of the ages to put away sin by the sacrifice of Himself (9:26)? It cannot be denied that all these acts are priestly acts and, insofar as they took place on earth, make it hard to understand how the writer can, as unqualifiedly as he does, assign the priestly ministry to the sphere of heaven. It has been suggested as a solution of this difficulty, that the author distinguishes between two orders of the priesthood in both of which Christ successively officiated, first the order of Aaron, next the order of Melchizedek. But nothing that is said in the Epistle really supports such a view. It would be impossible to point out in what respect the priestly ministry of Jesus connected with His death fell short of being a ministry after the order of Melchizedek. If, as is necessary, the essence of the latter be found in its eternity, then this character cannot be denied to the offering He made of Himself on Calvary, since plainly an everlasting effect is ascribed to it. It was eternal in its absoluteness, its spiritual nature, its reference to the heavenly world. Even in point of time the predicate of endless duration was not lacking to the ministry exercised by Jesus on earth. His death afforded no reason for regarding it as terminated or suspended, for in and through the death itself it was from the writer's own point of view continued on its uninterrupted course by means of the indissolvable life of the Son of God (7:16). In dying and in being dead the Son of God remained a priest forever. The distinction also violently separates, by assigning to two separate orders of priesthood, the two stages of the offering which the Epistle conceives of as most intimately and organically united, the offering upon the cross and the offering before the throne of God in heaven. The latter is based on and derives its efficacy from the former; hence they must belong to the same ministry: the Melchizedek-character could not inhere in the heavenly priesthood, unless it were also inherent in the sacrifice of Calvary. Obviously then the explanation required must be sought along a different line. And again we may find it in this, that the author determines the sphere to which Christ's priesthood belongs according to his view concerning the location of its center of gravity. Since this center of gravity lies in the act of bringing near to God, and not in the preparatory operations which were necessary for its accomplishment, the priesthood must have its true home where the approach to God is effected. And this is nowhere else than in the heavenly sanctuary. Perhaps the author's point of view in the matter may best be illustrated by a comparison with the one office of the Old Testament ritual which has most powerfully influenced his conception of our Lord's priestly work. This is the office performed by the high priest on the day of atonement, which constituted, as a matter of fact, the culmination of the sacrificial system. Now in this ministry of the day of atonement, prefiguring to an exceptional degree of exactness the high priestly ministry of Christ, the center plainly lay in the high priest's appearance before the face of Jehovah in the most holy place. This and no other act differentiated the task of the high priest from that of every other servant of the tabernacle. He and he alone could thus come near to God and representatively bring the people near. Therefore the place of his priesthood was emphatically the holy of holies, not the first tabernacle, far less the court. It might have been truly said that he officiated and could officiate nowhere else than there, and that if he had had to minister in the other compartments of the tabernacle, he would not have been a high priest at all, since ordinary priests and Levites performed this service leaving nothing distinctive that he could have claimed as his own. And yet, in the law of the day of atonement it is explicitly prescribed that the high priest must with his own hand slay the sacrificial animal in the court (Lev. 16:15). Of course this was not a menial act, which might just as well have been performed by somebody else; it was in the strictest sense of the word a highpriestly act, though from the nature of the case it could not be performed in the high priest's own specific sanctuary. Now it is altogether probable that the author of Hebrews looked upon the sacrifice of Christ on the cross as exactly corresponding to this act which by the hand of the high priest on the day of atonement took place in the court before the altar of burnt-offering. And since this single act of the high priest in the court does not prevent the Old Testament from assigning him to the holy of holies as the one true scene of his ministry, where alone this can develop its consummate function, so the single act of self-offering by Christ on the earthly mountain does not prevent the author from affirming that His priesthood belongs to heaven as the only sphere where it can truly accomplish its highest purpose, the bringing of the sacrifice and those for whom it is offered near to God. Finally, we must not overlook the part which the factor of personality plays in the shaping of the environment of the priestly office of Christ. This factor in general imparts to our Lord's priesthood a unique character and power. He carried into His office according to the

Epistle the eternal resources of the Son of God. He was made priest according to the dynamic of an indissolvable life. But the same principle would also affect the question of the locality of priesthood and of sacrifice. In the New Covenant the heavenly eternal world projects itself into this lower sphere. Even of believers it is true that they have now come to the heavenly city and stand in real connection through faith with the congregation above. If this applies to believers in general, how much more will it apply to Jesus, who not merely is the captain and finisher of faith, but who also, in virtue of His divine nature, continued to be part of the celestial order of things wherever He might abide in space. What He did was determined as to its local appurtenance by what He was. He created His own environment. It was within the boundaries of His own personality that the sacrifice was made. Through eternal Spirit He offered Himself up to God, and therefore the acts of His priesthood, though spacially taking place on earth, really belonged to the sphere of the αἰώνιον. Its ideal reference was not to any earthly order of priesthood but to the ministry in heaven for which it proved the necessary basis. Of Calvary it might have been said what Jacob said of Bethel: "This is none other than a house of God, this is the gate of heaven".

It will now have become clear, that the ideas of the priesthood and the covenant interlock no less closely than those of the covenant and revelation. The priesthood fulfills itself in being and bringing near to God and the purpose of the covenant is precisely the same. Both look to communion with God. There is no risk in affirming that the author was clearly conscious of this parallelism. The priesthood is to him center and substance of the covenant, that in which the covenant actually subsists. Both from the instrumental point of view of the covenant, and from the point of view of its eternal permanence, this holds true. As the covenant is an instrument of salvation, so is the priesthood. In the seventh chapter the comparison between the two orders of priesthood, the Levitical priesthood of the Old Testament and the Melchizedek priesthood of the New, turns with perfect naturalness into a comparison of the two covenants. In no other way than through the priesthood can the covenant as an instrument accomplish its purpose. The old Latin name "instrumentum" as a rendering for διαθήκη was from this point of view most felicitously chosen. The author is so thoroughly convinced of the central place of the priesthood in both dispensations that in 7:11 he even represents the Levitical priesthood as the higher category under which the whole law is subsumed: "Under it the people received the law". The entire legislation was grouped around it. The same thought finds formal expression a little later (verse 12) in the statement: "Where there is a change of priesthood there is made of necessity a change also of the law". The reason is not, as some think, that the law regulates the priesthood, and that consequently a change in the latter proves the former to have become invalidated. The author means it in the opposite sense: the priesthood, being changed, becomes a center from which the transformation of the religious system radiates in every direction. Hence also it is not a question of the new priest being another person individually considered, but a question of His being differently constituted; He is not merely ἄλλος but ἕτερος, heterogeneous in character, and this explains why with His arrival on the scene the old order must pass away. It is a small thing that in the point of priestly genealogy the rule has been changed, descent from Levi no longer being required; the great revolutionary fact is that in the place of a priest deriving his position from legal appointment consisting in a carnal, that is a perishable, commandment, there arises a priest who owes His office to the power of an endless life. Still in another form the same thought recurs in the twentieth verse. Here the difference between the Levitical priests and Jesus is said to appear in this, that they were made priests without an oath, He with an oath. The two priesthoods are different at their very source, the one flows from a legal ordinance, the other from an oath, and the oath has in it all the determination and all the energies of a supreme divine undertaking. In the legal ordinance God expresses His authority, in the oath He pledges Himself with the fulness of His prestige, and all His divine resources. There fore the oath-begotten priesthood is incomparably superior to the other. But, because the priesthood makes the covenant, the author draws straightway from the rôle played by the oath in His appointment the conclusion that Jesus is the surety of an intrinsically better covenant; thus once more confirming the rule that the excellence of the covenant is in exact proportion to the excellence of the priesthood. The synonymous terms "surety" and "mediator" also mark the interdependence of the priesthood and the covenant, for it is precisely as priest that Jesus becomes the surety, the sponsor of the New Covenant: because He is an oath-appointed priest He is a better surety. Through the manner of His priesthood He renders the effectuation of the covenant assured.

If the priesthood of Jesus is thus seen to be the heart of the instrumental covenant, it occupies the same place in the covenant as a permanent reality. This aspect of the matter finds expression in 12:24: among the eternal possessions to which believers have come in the heavenly Jerusalem the author here assigns the highest place to Jesus and that in His capacity of mediator of the New Covenant. Both the covenant and the priesthood retain in the eternal world their abiding significance. In the eternal priest the covenant has become eternalized. For this reason the blood with which Jesus was brought back from the dead, that is the expiation which in His endless resurrection-life He makes available, is called the blood of an everlasting covenant, and in virtue of it Jesus never ceases to be the great Shepherd of the sheep of the. Israel of God.

The equivalence of the priesthood to the covenant will become still more clearly apparent if we trace the formative influence of the one upon the other in the Epistle's descriptions of the subjective religious life of believers. This life is frequently referred to in terms directly drawn from, or at least colored by, the priestly conception. These terms all attach themselves not to the intermediate, preparatory stage of the priesthood, but to the final act in which the priesthood issues, which shows once more how firmly the author's interest in the priesthood is centered there. A standing name for believers as benefited by the priesthood of Christ is "those who draw near". "Having then a great high priest … let us draw near with boldness unto the throne of grace" (4:14–16). Jesus, by virtue of His eternal priesthood "is able to save to the uttermost them that draw near unto God through Him" (7:25). And the writer exhorts the readers: "Having a great priest over the house of God, let us draw near with a true heart in fulness of faith". This, it will be seen, is terminology drawn from the official life of the priest: it is his business to draw near; the people through his work are enabled to do after him what he has first done alone. By thus being transferred to the daily covenant-life of every believer, the description imparts to the latter a peculiarly active, mobile character; its distinguishing feature is not merely to stand in communion with God, but to tend, to draw towards God in an ever renewed approach. The resemblance becomes even more pronounced when not only the movement of drawing near but also the act of offering up

is transferred from the priest to the Christian: "Through
Him then let us offer up a sacrifice of praise to God
continually, that is the fruit of lips that make confession to
His name" (13:15). This assumes a still more generalized
form when the Christian life is called a λατρεία a "service".
As the word in the original shows, we must keep away from
this conception all the modern associations of altruistic
endeavor in the cause of God: it stands strictly for the
service of worship which directly terminates upon God. It
too has been taken from the ritual vocabulary of the Old
Testament. Of the priests it is said that they "serve" in the
tabernacle. "They that draw near", and "they that serve" are
used in entirely the same connections to describe believers
in their central religious occupation (9:9; 10:1). The
purifying of Christ's blood is for this purpose that believers
may be enabled by it "to serve the living God". It does this
because it cleanses the conscience from dead works, i.e.
from the defilement of sin, and thus restores to the sinner
the privilege of appearing as a worshipper before the face of
God (9:14). It ought to be observed, however, that the
Epistle does not go so far in this direction as the Old
Testament representation of the covenant-status of Israel on
the one hand, and on the other, in dependence on it, the
First Epistle of Peter and the Apocalypse do, when they
definitely invest the people of God with priestly character.
In placing the covenant before Israel Jehovah promised them
that under it they would be a kingdom of priests, a holy

nation, in other words that in their collective capacity they would sustain to Him the same relation that a priest sustains to the deity in whose temple he ministers (Ex. 19:6). Peter transfers this to the New Testament congregation, addressing his readers as "a holy priesthood, to offer up spiritual sacrifices through Jesus Christ" (1 Pet. 2:5). And the seer of the Apocalypse bases a doxology upon the fact that Christ has made believers joint-kings and priests with Himself and God, or priests of God and of Christ (1:6; 5:10; 20:6). But to the writer of our Epistle, the priesthood of Jesus has assumed such stupendous proportions and been brought into such close connection with His divine sonship and with His specifically redemptive function that he naturally hesitates to include believers in its exercise even after a secondary and metaphorical fashion. Still upon the fundamental duty of the believer to make his whole covenant-life a worship-service of God he insists. At this point the opposite pole of the διαθήκη -conception, that representing the sovereignty and majesty of God, exerts its influence. As in the making of the covenant there is no absolute twosidedness, the divine prerogative being paramount, so in the resulting covenant-intercourse there can be no absolute coequality; the fellowship with God which stands at the goal inevitably assumes the form of a service, a worship of God by man. It is covenant-communion exercised in a sanct-everything that enters the stamp of His own majesty and dominion. The covenant-life

of Israel concentrated in the uary, where God alone is
supreme and where He sets upon tabernacle already bore
this character; it belongs in a heightened degree to the
covenant-life of the New Testament church, but its
fundamental significance is best seen from this, that it
remains the constitutive principle of the eschatological
congregation, whose component orders are enumerated
according to the rank they occupy in the heavenly service of
God. No small part of the practical value of the Epistle
consists in the great energy with which it upholds the direct
Godward function of worship as lying at the very basis of
Christianity. Hebrews is the Epistle of the cultus and the
Christian life it portrays is a cultus in the noblest sense of the
word. At a time when the man-ward functions of religion
are in the ascendant, especially when the word "service" is
being almost monopolized for the Christian activities that
aim at the promotion of the wellbeing of man, it can do no
harm to let ourselves be reminded by the writer of this
Epistle that there is such a thing as a service to God that is
not rendered by indirection, but is as exclusively and
directly appropriated to Him as the gift that is laid upon the
altar, an alabaster-vase of ointment whose very preciousness
consists in this that it cannot even be sold and the proceeds
given to the poor. It will be said perhaps that the cult-
terminology employed by the Epistle in the description of
the Christian life is a mere transparent allegory, occasioned
by speaking of the New Covenant in terms of the Old, and
that therefore no positive significance can be attached to it

except that of a momentary accommodation to the exigencies of the argument, or possibly to the Jewish-Christian standpoint of the readers, who would be pleased to find in the Christian institutions a reflex of their own ancestral rites. This explanation is hardly adequate, partly because it is far from certain that the Epistle is addressed to Jewish-Christian readers, but mainly for another reason. The Old Testament ceremonial institutions were to the author not matter-of-fact customs such as this theory of accommodation assumes; they were to him the product of revelation in the strictest sense of the word; that they were revealed involved on his premises, as we have seen, the embodiment in them of everlasting principles of religion; therefore the cult-aspect in which he represents Christianity reproduces in his opinion these same principles, which amounts to saying that it is more than a form, that it represents something inseparable from the Christian religion. The best proof of the soundness of this position lies in the eschatological use which the Epistle makes of the same terminology. The language of priest and altar and sacrifice and cultus is transferred to the consummate, heavenly state; this would not have been possible had the author looked upon all such forms of statement as pure symbolism. His intense spiritualism should not be confounded with idealism. It is opposed only to materialism, not to the sound realism which the New Testament writings everywhere uphold with reference to the future world. It may be difficult for us, and probably would have been difficult for the writer, to define

in the concrete what exactly is meant by the higher
tabernacle not made with hands, not of this creation; by the
heavenly altar; by the appearance of Christ before the face of
God; by the cleansing of the things above; but human
inability to form of this any other than a sense-conception
does not warrant the inference that, where sense is
excluded, all objectivity disappears and that everything
taught of the heavenly life may be safely dissolved into
internal processes and mental states. No, the archetypes of
these things are real to the author; he believes in the
concrete objective existence of the contents of the celestial
life, though the wings on which he soars to it are of the
finest, most ethereal spirituality. And, inasmuch as the
Christian life on earth anticipates the conditions of the world
to come, it likewise must needs bear the impress of the
eternal moulds into which it will be cast hereafter.

Still another respect in which the covenant and the
priestly conception have jointly put their stamp upon the
Epistle's view of the Christian life may be briefly touched
upon in this connection. It is characteristic of covenant and
priesthood alike that they emphasize the collective no less
than the individual status of the religious subject. This
follows directly from the preceding point. If Christianity is a
worship, a service offered to God, then it must organize
itself on a collective basis, for the worship of God cannot
fulfill itself unless it proceeds from the congregation as a
whole. In fact the Old Testament *berith* and the Old

Testament priesthood had this very thing as their main purpose, that a proper cultus should be offered to Jehovah through the providing of a proper cult-unit in the congregation of Israel. Not merely the individual Israelite has to render this service; the people are obligated to it and responsible for it. On its behalf the regular sacrifices are offered and the regular offices of worship discharged. Hence Paul represents the λατρεία or "service" as one of the great distinctive privileges of Israel, coördinate with such things as the adoption, the Shechinah, the διαθῆκα. the giving of the law, the promises, the fathers, and the giving birth, after the flesh, to the Christ (Rom. 9:4, 5). The writer of Hebrews transfers this collective manner of speaking to the New Testament. He speaks in a number of passages of Christians as constituting "the people", "the people of God" (2:17; 4:9; 8:10; 13:12), just as he applies this name to the Old Testament Israel (5:3; 7:5, 11, 27; 9:7, 19; 10:30; 11:25). It is a mistake to draw from this an argument for the Jewish extraction of the readers of the Epistle, as if the writer meant that from a racial, national point of view they form the continuation of the people of Israel. With bodily descent this whole way of speaking has nothing whatever to do. It is not an ethnic but a theocratic designation. Even in regard to the Old Testament Israel, where the author introduces it, he is not led to do so by the thought of their common physical descent. Israel in the last analysis became a λαός, a people of God, because Jehovah in the *berith* organized them as a congregation for His service. And so it is under the New Covenant. It will be observed that in most of the passages where the terms "people", "people of God" occur, their mention has been induced by the connection of the statement with the covenant or priesthood. Jesus makes expiation for the sins of the people (2:17). There remains a Sabbath-keeping for the people of God (4:9). Jesus suffered that He might sanctify the people with His blood (13:12). The high-priest offers for sin both for himself and for the people (5:3; 7:27; 9:7). The Levitical priests take the tithes of the people (7:5). Moses sprinkled the people (9:19). The representative position which the priest occupies with reference to the beneficiaries of His office of itself brings about the consolidation of these into a people of God.

Another name for the body of believers is "the house of God". This also is connected with the idea of the priesthood, for Jesus is called in one of the passages where it occurs "a great priest over the house of God" (10:21). In this name "house of God" the principle of organic continuity of grace is implied, which elsewhere in the New Testament and throughout the Old appears as one of the important correlates of the covenant-conception. If God enters into the covenant relation not with men in their individual capacity only but as members of a priestly organism, then the perpetuation of this organism is ipso facto provided for. The Old Testament emphasizes throughout that Jehovah establishes His covenant not merely with the parents but

with their offspring in the successive generations. Both Peter
in his speeches in Acts (2:39; 3:25) and Paul in Galatians
(4:24–31) represent the covenant as a procreative organism,
having its sons and daughters through the ages of redemptive
history. It must be acknowledged, however, that this side of
the matter, while doubtless implied, is not made explicitly
prominent in the Epistle. Apart from the covenant idea the
element of continuity is found by the writer inherent in the
promises given to Abraham. These promises he does not call
a covenant, for the old διαθήκη, with which the new is
coördinated, begins according to his representation at Sinai,
not with Abraham. But the promise underlies the whole
subsequent development; it is the broad basis on which the
two successive covenants rest; New Testament believers
have an equal interest in it with the saints of the old
dispensation, and in this way uninterrupted continuity of
grace is recognized (6:13–18).

We have now traced the influence of the covenant-idea in
the Epistle along the two lines of revelation and of
priesthood. It is easy to see that these lines represent two
mutually complementary movements, each beginning at the
point opposite to that from which the other proceeds, and
having for their common destination the realization of
fellowship between God and man. In revelation God makes
His approach to man; through the priesthood man makes His
approach to God; where both reach their ideal perfection,
there the ideal covenant is given. The covenant movement

must necessarily flow through these two channels. And, since Hebrews makes the covenant-idea central, by far the larger part of what it has to teach concerning the interplay of religion between God and man attaches itself to these two conceptions. Still there is an element in the description of the subjective side of religion in the Epistle which shows no outward and formal dependence upon the idea of the covenant. This element is found largely in the account given by the author of the patriarchal history, of the annals of faith during the period when the old Sinaitic covenant was not yet in existence. And the interesting feature of this description is, that, while the formal notion of the covenant plays no part whatever in it, yet the same outstanding and characteristic traits which the account of the later religious life assumes under the influence of the covenant-conception appear in it with striking distinctness. The significance of this phenomenon lies in the witness it bears to the inherence of the covenant form in the very idea of religion itself as the writer conceives it. Religion is to his view so essentially and so inevitably a matter of mutual union and fellowship in the conscious sphere, that its manner of appearance and mode of exercise cannot help suggesting the thought of the covenant even where there is no conscious desire on the writer's part to obtrude it upon our attention. The description of faith in the eleventh chapter is well-adapted to illustrate this. Faith is not here set forth from the specifically Pauline point of view as saving trust in Christ as the exponent of the grace and power of God. At first sight it may even seem to possess far less personal concentration than the Pauline conception of faith. The author defines it in an impersonal way as "assurance of things hoped for, conviction of things not seen" (11:1). And yet that this is more so in appearance than in reality follows from the other eminently personal statement: "Without faith it is impossible to be pleasing unto God, for he that cometh unto God must believe that He is, and that He is a rewarder of them that seek after Him" (verse 6). Though faith is the organ of perception of the unseen and future realities and takes in with its vision a comprehensive realm of objects, there is in this circle which it sweeps a center, a focus; the things not seen and the things hoped for have a true unity, and this unity lies in God. No greater mistake could be made than to imagine, that the faith illustrated in this chapter is no more than the innate human faculty to believe in things that cannot be perceived by the senses. The heroes of this faith are the great figures of the history of redemption, and this of itself proves that its objects are the supernatural realities of the world of redemption—whence also hope is a species of faith. Though not in the specific Pauline sense of justifying faith, it is saving faith no less than the faith preached by Paul. And it is furthermore portrayed by the author as in the highest degree an intensive faith for the reason that at the time when it was exercised the redemptive realities had not yet been manifested, and all sight, all concrete experience and enjoyment of these realities was absent. All these died not having obtained. It was a faith that, subjectively speaking, had nothing but itself to fall back upon. This, however, is but another way of saying that it was faith in the promises. Now faith in a promise can from the nature of the case have no other than a pointedly personal reference. Belief in the fulfilment of the promise can only rest in trust in the promising Person. A personal occupation of the religious consciousness with God who stood back of the promises was therefore essential to the faith of the patriarchs. Only the author gives this occupation a far wider range than the line of reasoning just followed would seem to require. Faith in the fulfilment of a promise might be concerned only with the veracity of the one who gave it and hence might lead to personal touch with Him only at this single point of His character. The Epistle means far more than that the patriarchs relied on the truthfulness of God. Its view is rather this, that through the absence of the concrete temporal gifts of salvation the patriarchs were brought to an immanent apprehension of the source of these gifts in the character of God Himself, and that not along the line of the divine faithfulness alone but in a most comprehensive manner along the line of all the elements that the nature of God as revealed to them contained. Having naught but promises their faith was stimulated to approach the content of salvation on its ideal side as it lay in God, the expression of His mind, His purpose, His nature with reference to them. The proximate result of this was a strong spiritualization of their religious life. The promise, the word, is the most spiritual form in which the gifts of God can be apprehended. The next result showed itself in that otherworldliness or heavenly-mindedness which the author has so beautifully portrayed in his account of the character of Abraham. The patriarchs confessed that they were strangers and pilgrims on the earth: and this was because they could see and greet the promises only from afar. It is evident from this form of statement that their faith did not rest in the historical satisfaction that it might obtain by projecting itself through the vista of time to the point of fulfilment. On the contrary, because the vista was long and their faith eager, it made the sublime leap to the heavenly eternal things; to the seeing, the greeting of the promises from afar, there was added the seeking of a better country. And it is important to notice how the author represents this ascent of the patriarchs' faith to the heavenly world as in no way mediated by the typical fulfilment of the promise that was to intervene between them and its final New Testament realization. The ascent to the heavenly country did not use as a stepping-stone the thought of the earthly Canaan; it was made directly from the vantage ground of the promises of God. It greeted from afar the Christ and drew near to the heavenly country above; in sublime sacrifice it surrendered whatever of earthly developments lay between. In this close touch and intense pre-occupation of the patriarchs with the celestial world, the Epistle almost seems to find a sort of preëxistence of the Christian relation to the same world, something of the same directness of approach to it and of the same absorption by its interests that the New Covenant has brought and which were unknown to the intermediate period when believers were dependent on shadows. As Paul found in the patriarchal period the preformation of the religion of grace and of universalism which the law coming in after could only obscure but not abrogate, so the author of Hebrews finds in it an earlier stage of that thorough spiritual-mindedness and of that profound other-worldliness of Christianity which it was his specific task to set forth.

Even this, however, is not yet the highest aspect in which the Epistle invites us to consider the faith of the patriarchs. As spirituality led to heavenly-mindedness, so heavenly-mindedness in its turn assumes the form of a personal attachment to God. As the spiritual and the heavenly are to the author at bottom identical, so of both the center of attraction lies in God. Faith in its last analysis was to the patriarchs the apprehension, the possession, the enjoyment of God Himself. Throughout the music of this chapter the dominance of the personal note makes itself distinctly heard. Those who looked for the city that has the foundations sought it for no other reason than that its maker and builder is God. It is because it is the city of God, the structure in which He has embodied His own perfection, in which His thoughts and purposes for His own stand objectified, that it forms a worthy object of the supreme religious quest of the believer. In it is God at every point and those who dwell in it see His face continually. The measure of their desire for it becomes the measure of their love of God. Herein also lies

the defense against the charge that otherworldliness is a
sickly strain in the religious consciousness, because inspired
by selfish, eudaemonistic motives and because apt to hinder
the development of a wholesome interest in and faithful
performance of the duties of the present life. This would be
so if it were anything else but God-centered. The root of
that is ugly and injurious in extreme eschatological
preoccupation can always be traced back to this, that it is
insufficiently religious, that people seek something else in
other world than the perfect union with and service of God.
Hence the two widely different types of other-worldliness
that go side by side through religious history, the one
disappointed with present conditions for self's sake and
projecting into the future or into heaven the quenching of its
own unpurified desires, and therefore apt to show itself
times of spiritual decline or secular adversity; the other
unsatisfied because the highest religious experience in this
life cannot still a thirst for the living God that has capacities
made for the world to come, and therefore apt to appear in
times of deep and pure religious revival. The eschatological
interest of the early church was very keen, but it prevailingly
of the latter kind. So far as the authoritative teaching of the
New Testament books is concerned, it consistently
emphasizes the thought that what believers seek in the world
to come is the perfection of their religious relation to God.
Where any lower motive came into play, as among the new
converts who as yet were but imperfect Christianized could
not fail to happen, and where the acute belief in the nearness

of the end or the sharp disappointment at its delay, threatened to interfere with the normal conduct of the life of the present, the needful corrective was immediately applied, and it consisted always in this that an appeal was made to the Christian's allegiance to God, whom to love and whom to serve should be his supreme concern alike in this world and in the world to come. We can observe this very thing in our Epistle. Several indications point to the existence among the readers of an eschatological preoccupation which was largely concerned with externals and which, when the external developments failed to come as quickly as had been expected, gave rise to discontent and through discontent to unbelief. It is in order to correct this evil that the author shifts the emphasis from the external to the internal, that he spiritualizes the content of the future life, and that in spiritualizing it he puts its center in the believer's desire for God, all of which enabled him to show that in principle the treasures of the world to come are not shut up in an inapproachable future but lie now and here open to the experience of the Christian. Hope is made a species of faith and faith is encouraged to enter in and lay hold upon what is behind the veil. Through this whole noble description of faith rings the note of personal attachment, covenant-loyalty to God. It is a faith through which, like Moses, the Christian can endure as seeing Him who is invisible, which chooses rather to share ill-treatment with a people that belongs to God, than to inherit the treasures of Egypt. It is the responsive act on the believer's part to the act of covenant-

committal on the part of God. Religion consummates itself
in a mutual avowal, the people bearing God's reproach and
offering up a sacrifice of praise to Him continually, even the
fruit of lips that make confession to His name, and God not
being ashamed to be called their God and preparing for them
a city. Thus the Epistle's idea of faith falls into line with its
teaching on revelation and on the priesthood and back of all
three equally is seen to lie the covenantal conception of
religion.

With this result we may consider ourselves to have
reached the conclusion of the task set for our enquiry. It is a
noble view of Christianity that the Epistle holds up to us.
The writer unites profound historical grasp of the organic
development of redemption with keen theological insight
into the unchanging essence of revealed religion and fine
psychological feeling for the generic forms which it assumes
when entering into the conscious experience of man. In all
these respects the teaching of Hebrews has done its full share
in laying the foundations on which the later structure of
Christian doctrine has been reared, a more generous share
perhaps than, judging from its compass, might have been
expected. And in no other theology have the principles that
shape the Epistle been so fully and faithfully incorporated as
in that produced by the Reformed churches. We do not
mean by this that the Reformed theology is to a large extent,
like that of Hebrews, a covenant-theology, for that might be
a matter of mere superficial resemblance. It is not that the

label or the bottles are the same; the wine is the same in both cases. In some measure this may be explainable from the fact that the representatives of the federal theology drew upon Hebrews as their source. On the whole, however, we have to do here not with a slavish borrowing of material but with a free and living reproduction of identical principles. Both in Hebrews and with the Reformed teachers a peculiar insight into the highest possibilities of religion instinctively chose for its form of expression the covenant-idea.

It may be briefly pointed out how in the Reformed theology the same great perceptions lie embedded that we have found shaping the doctrine of the Epistle. The first place should be given to the recognition of the majesty and sovereignty of God in the whole process of religion and redemption. It is all embraced in a διαθήκη, a comprehensive system, and in this system all things are of God. His is the originality in conceiving, His the initiative in inaugurating, His the monergism in carrying out. There is no room for any fortuitousness of chance, any uncertainty of issue, no point anywhere where the hand of God is not in absolute control. It is a system that has an oath of God and a sponsorship of Christ back of all its provisions. And the principle thus recognized in the redemptive sphere also asserts itself in the general religious attitude of man towards God. A deep impression of the divine majesty colors all intercourse with Him. For Him are all things and through Him are all things. The creature exists for His sake. He is the living God into whose hands it is fearful to fall, for those who disobey Him a consuming fire. A consciousness of strict accountability in view of God's sovereign rights over man has always characterized the Reformed religion even to such an extent as to invite the charge that its puritanic practice savors of a spirit of legalism more at home in the Old Testament than in the New. But legalism has nothing to do with this; it is here as in Hebrews simply the correlate in life of the vivid impression of the majesty of God in belief. Legalism lacks the supreme sense of worship. It obeys but it does not adore. And no deeper notes of adoration have ever been struck than those inspired by the Reformed faith, no finer fruit of the lips making confession to God's name has ever been placed upon the Christian altar.

In the second place, and as in a sense counterbalancing the foregoing, we may notice the stress laid in Reformed doctrine upon the directness and spirituality and intimacy of the intercourse of God with the soul of the believer. The supreme contact is made not in the mystical regions of the unconscious, nor through magical sacramentarian processes, but in the luminous sphere of conscious fellowship through the interchange of thought and affection. The God who dwells in the high and holy place comes nearest to the humble heart and the contrite spirit. This is not saying that it is unworthy of God to touch and influence man on the subconscious side. It only implies that such contact and influence are always a means to an end, not religious ends in themselves. The religious process tends to vision in the light, to knowledge face to face, precisely because it has to interact with and form part of the life of Him who is a light and in whom there is no darkness at all. For this reason the ultimate root of every believer's relation to God lies in the most intimate and individual act of election, an act wherein the love of God consciously chooses and sets up over against itself a human spirit to be bound to God in the bonds of everlasting friendship. Election and the covenants answer to each other as the root and the fruitage of the highest type of religion.

In the third place the Reformed Theology ascribes to the Christian life a unique degree of devotion to the interests and the glory of God. The believer does not merely desire to have intercourse with God, but specifically to make this intercourse subservient to glorifying God. Hence on the one hand the high place which the direct worship of God holds in the exercise of the religious function, on the other hand the consistent effort to organize the whole of life on the principle of a comprehensive service of God, the religious impulse imparting to every human activity and achievement that spirit by which they are made to redound to the honoring of God's name. No brighter examples of absolute devotion and self-surrender to God in unstinted covenant service can be found anywhere than in the annals of the Reformed faith.

In the fourth place the Reformed Theology has with greater earnestness than any other type of Christian doctrine upheld the principles of the absoluteness and unchanging, identity of truth. It is the most anti-pragmatic of all forms of Christian teaching. And this is all the more remarkable since it has from the beginning shown itself possessed of a true historic sense in the apprehension of the progressive character of the deliverance of truth. Its doctrine of the covenants on its historical side represents, the first attempt at constructing a history of revelation and may justly be considered the precursor of what is at present called Biblical Theology. But the Reformed have always insisted upon it that at no point shall recognition of the historical delivery and apprehension of truth be permitted to degenerate into a relativity of truth. The history remains a history of revelation. Its total product agrees absolutely in every respect with the sum of truth as it lies in the eternal mind and purpose of God. If already the religion of the Old and New Testament Church was identical, while the process of supernatural revelation was still going on, how much more must the church, since God has spoken for the last time in His Son, uphold the ideal absoluteness of her faith as guaranteed by its agreement with the Word of God that abideth forever. It is an unchristian and an unbiblical procedure to make development superior to revelation instead of revelation superior to development, to accept belief and tendencies as true because they represent the spirit of the time and in a superficial optimism may be regarded as making for progress. Christian cognition is not an evolution of truth, but a fallible apprehension of truth which must at each point be tested by an accessible absolute norm of truth. To take one's stand upon the infallibility of the Scriptures is an eminently religious act; it honors the supremacy of God in the sphere of truth in the same way as the author of Hebrews does by insisting upon it, notwithstanding all progress, that the Old and the New Testament are the same authoritative speech of God. In these four vital respects we may truthfully say that the covenant theology has the high credentials of being in agreement with the lines along which the covenant idea is worked out in Hebrews. And, insofar as this is the case, it is not an unimportant variation, but a reversion to type, in which the conception of the Christian life comes nearest to one, and that not the least attractive, of the forms in which it is portrayed in the New Testament.